There Is More Moving Beyond Cultural
Christianity to a Life of Purpose, Passion,
and Power

There Is More Moving Beyond Cultural Christianity to a Life of Purpose, Passion, and Power

William Brunson

There Is More

2

There Is More
Moving Beyond Cultural Christianity
to a Life of Purpose, Passion, and Power
Dr. Bill Brunson

4 |

There Is More: Moving Beyond Cultural Christianity to a Life of Purpose, Passion, and Power

Unless otherwise indicated, all Scripture quotations are taken from the Holy Bible, New International Version®, NIV®.

Copyright © 1973, 1978, 1984, 2011 by Biblica, Inc.™
Used by permission. All rights reserved worldwide.
ISBN: 979-8-9943813-1-1
Printed in the United States of America
First Edition: 2025

DEDICATION

This book is dedicated to Michelle – my wife and co-adventurer in all of life.

CONTENTS

INTRODUCTION

THE INVITATION

When Jesus Says "Follow Me," What Does He Actually Mean?

It wasn't an interview. They didn't ask for a benefits package.

There was no negotiation about vacation time, no questions about work-life balance, no request for a detailed job description. Simon Peter and his brother Andrew were hauling in their nets when a rabbi from Nazareth said two words that would change everything: "Follow Me."

Matthew's Gospel tells us what happened next: "At once they left their nets and followed him" (Matthew 4:20, NIV). Not after sleeping on it. Not after consulting their financial advisor. Not after checking their calendars. At once.

A few steps down the shoreline, Jesus found James and John in a boat with their father Zebedee, mending nets. Same invitation. Same response. "Immediately they left the boat and their father and followed him" (Matthew 4:22, NIV). They walked away from their family business, their inheritance, their entire future—all for a man they barely knew.

Here's what I want you to notice: Jesus didn't offer them a comfortable add-on to their existing lives. He didn't say, "Hey, when you're done fishing, swing by the synagogue and we'll chat about spiritual things." He didn't invite them to attend His teaching sessions when it was convenient. He called them to leave everything behind and step into an entirely new existence.

I've read the Gospel accounts over and over throughout the years. So, I can confidently say that there's no record anywhere in Scripture of Jesus saying, "Follow Me when it fits your schedule" or "Add Me to your life when and where you have margin." From the very beginning, discipleship has meant one thing: surrender.

And that's the question this book asks: What if Jesus meant what He said?

The Problem We Don't Want to Talk About

Somewhere along the way, we did something to the gospel that would have been unrecognizable to those first disciples.

We domesticated it.

We took the Lion of Judah—the One who overturned tables in the temple, who stared down Pharisees, who marched deliberately toward a cross—and we turned Him into something safe. Something manageable. Something that fits neatly into a Sunday morning routine without making too many demands on Monday through Saturday.

We turned following Jesus into simply believing in Jesus, as if intellectual agreement were the same thing as walking away from our nets. We decided that it is sufficient to be fans of Jesus – pro Jesus – claiming to be on his side. We made Christianity about getting fire insurance for the afterlife rather than experiencing a revolution in this life. We reduced the kingdom of God to a list of dos and don'ts, then convinced ourselves we were doing pretty well because we checked most of the boxes.

German pastor and theologian Dietrich Bonhoeffer saw this coming. Writing from Nazi Germany in the 1930s, he warned about what he called "cheap grace"—the kind of grace we give ourselves that asks nothing of us. Grace without discipleship. Grace without transformation. Grace that leaves us exactly as it found us.

Bonhoeffer paid for his convictions with his life, executed in a concentration camp just weeks before Germany surrendered. But his warning still echoes: when we separate grace from following Jesus, we lose both. Cheap grace isn't really grace at all—it's self-deception dressed up in religious language.

I've been a pastor for over thirty-five years, and I've watched too many people settle for this diminished version of the Christian life. They show up on Sundays, put a check in the offering plate (or set up a minimal amount to be drafted), try to be nice to their neighbors, and genuinely believe they're living out their faith. They're not bad people—far from it. They're often the backbone of our churches. But there's a restlessness in them that shows up when we're honest with each other.

"Is this all there is?"

"I feel like I'm going through the motions."

"Something's missing, but I can't put my finger on it."

If you've ever had those thoughts, this book is for you. Not to condemn you—God knows we've had enough condemnation in the church and in the world—but to invite you into something more. Something that looks a lot more like what Peter and Andrew experienced on that ordinary day that became extraordinary.

What Jesus Actually Offers

Here's the good news, and I mean that literally: Jesus doesn't just call us away from something. He calls us to something magnificent.

In John's Gospel, Jesus put it in unforgettable terms: "The thief comes only to steal and kill and destroy; I have come that they may have life, and have it abundantly, to the full, to the max." (John 10:10, NIV).

Abundant life, life to the full, life to the max. Not life that's half-lived. Not existence squeezed between obligations and exhaustion. Not the spiritual equivalent of treading water. Jesus offers a life so rich, so purpose-filled, so transformative that everything else looks thin by comparison.

Now, I need to be honest with you. "Life to the max" isn't code for "life without problems." The prosperity gospel preachers who promise health, wealth, and your best life now if you just have enough faith—they're selling something Jesus never offered. Peter, Andrew,

James, and John didn't walk away from their nets into a life of ease. They walked into hardship, persecution, and (all but one) eventually martyrdom.

But here's what they also walked into: purpose. Meaning. Joy that circumstances couldn't steal. The unshakeable knowledge that their lives mattered, that they were part of something eternal, that every day had significance because they were living for the only thing worth living for.

That's the life Jesus offers. It's not comfortable, but it's alive. It's not safe, but it's significant. It's not easy, but it's everything.

And here's the truth: the people who seem most alive aren't the ones with the easiest circumstances. They're the ones who've surrendered most completely. There's something about letting go—truly letting go—that unleashes a quality of life nothing else can produce.

This Isn't Something New

The call to total surrender didn't start with Jesus on the shores of Galilee. It echoes throughout Scripture, beginning long before that moment.

Think about Abraham. He was comfortable in Ur of the Chaldeans—established, secure, surrounded by family. Then God showed up with an absurd invitation: "Go from your country, your people and your father's household to the land I will show you" (Genesis 12:1, NIV). Notice what God didn't tell him - where he was going. Abraham had to leave everything familiar for a destination he'd learn about somewhere along the way.

What did Abraham do? "So, Abram went, as the Lord had told him" (Genesis 12:4, NIV). A simple phrase that changed human history. He didn't demand details. He didn't negotiate terms. He went.

Or consider Moses. He'd built a new life for himself in Midian—wife, kids, sheep to tend, a rhythm that worked. Then a bush caught fire and refused to burn out, and God had some ideas about Moses' retirement plans. Go back to Egypt. Confront the most powerful ruler on earth. Lead two million people through a wilderness. Moses had every excuse in the book: "I'm not qualified. I'm not eloquent. They won't believe me. Send someone else."

God didn't disagree with Moses' self-assessment. He just said, essentially, "I know. Go anyway. I'll be with you." And Moses went.

Then there's Ruth—a Moabite widow with every reason to stay in familiar territory. Her husband was dead. Her security was gone. Her mother-in-law Naomi was headed back to Israel with nothing to offer her. The sensible thing, the safe thing, would have been to stay in Moab, remarry, rebuild her life among her own people.

But Ruth said something that still takes my breath away: "Where you go, I will go, and where you stay, I will stay. Your people will be my people and your God my God" (Ruth 1:16, NIV). She chose covenant loyalty over security, faithfulness over comfort, surrender over self-preservation. And she ended up in the lineage of Jesus.

David. Rahab. Esther. Elijah. The Bible is full of ordinary people who became extraordinary not because of their abilities but because of their availability. They said yes when God called, even when the call didn't make sense, even when the cost was high, even when everything in them wanted to stay put.

This is the pattern. This is how God has always worked. He finds people who are willing to let go of what they're holding so they can grab hold of what He's offering. And what He's offering is always bigger than what they're releasing.

Where We're Headed Together

So, here's what I want to do in the pages ahead. I want to take you on a journey—the same journey those first disciples took, the same journey Abraham and Moses and Ruth took, the same journey countless followers of Jesus have taken throughout history.

We'll start by getting honest about where we are. In Chapter 1, we'll look in the mirror and ask some uncomfortable questions about cultural Christianity. Not to heap guilt on you—that's the last thing I want—but because you can't get somewhere new until you acknowledge where you're starting from.

Then we'll count the cost. Chapter 2 tackles the hard sayings of Jesus, the ones we often skip over because they make us squirm. Jesus never used bait-and-switch tactics. He told people upfront what following Him would require. We need to do the same honest reckoning.

In Chapter 3, we'll explore what surrender actually looks like—and what it produces. Here's the paradox you'll discover: surrender isn't about losing yourself. It's about finding yourself. When you let go of your agenda, your purpose emerges.

Chapter 4 takes us into community. Discipleship was never meant to be a solo project. The Acts 2 church gives us a blueprint for what transformed living looks like when it happens together—and it's breathtaking.

Finally, in Chapter 5, we'll step into mission. Disciples aren't just saved to sit—they're saved to serve. Every follower of Jesus has a role to play in God's redemptive purposes for the world. Finding that role isn't just a nice bonus; it's the whole point.

And then, in Chapter 6, we'll land somewhere important: a bold yes. A commitment. A decision to stop dabbling and start following for real.

Let me be clear about something before we go any further: this book isn't about perfection. I've been following Jesus for a long time, and I still blow it regularly. Discipleship isn't about achieving some spiritual performance standard. It's about direction. It's about movement. It's about saying yes to the greatest adventure available to any human being and keeping on saying yes, day after day, even when you stumble.

Grace is real. Jesus knows your limitations better than you do, and He's calling you anyway. The same Jesus who invited Peter—who would deny Him three times—to follow Him is inviting you. Not to perfect performance, but to a transforming relationship.

Running to Win: Eric Liddell's Story

I want to tell you about a man who understood the difference between cultural Christianity and surrendered discipleship—and lived it out on the world's biggest stage.

Eric Liddell was born in China to missionary parents but raised in Scotland, where he became one of the fastest men alive. In 1924, he was the overwhelming favorite to win the 100-meter dash at the Paris Olympics. This was his race. His moment. Everything he'd trained for.

Then he discovered that the 100-meter heats were scheduled for a Sunday.

Eric's conviction was that Sunday belonged to God, not to sports—not even Olympic sports. The pressure was enormous. The British Olympic Committee, the press, even members of the royal family tried to persuade him to run. National pride was at stake. This was his one shot at glory.

Eric wouldn't budge.

Instead, he entered the 400-meter race—an event he hadn't seriously trained for, four times longer than his specialty. By every reasonable calculation, he didn't have a chance.

Before the race, a trainer slipped a piece of paper into Eric's hand. On it was a quote from 1 Samuel: "Those who honor me I will honor." Eric went out and ran the race of his life, crossing the finish line in world-record time, arms thrown back, head tilted toward heaven.

The 1981 film "Chariots of Fire" made Eric famous all over again, and it includes a line that captures something essential about him. When his sister urged him to forget running and get serious about missionary work, Eric responded: "I believe God made me for a purpose—but He also made me fast. And when I run, I feel His pleasure."

That's the difference. A cultural Christian might have been a Christian athlete—faith as one identity among many. Eric Liddell was an athlete who happened to be completely surrendered to Christ. His faith wasn't an add-on to his running; it was the foundation beneath everything.

Here's what I find even more compelling than the Olympic story: after his moment of global triumph, Eric went back to China as a missionary. He could have cashed in on his fame for years. Instead, he spent the rest of his life serving in obscurity, eventually dying in a Japanese internment camp in 1945, just months before the war ended.

Those who knew him in that camp said that even there—sick, starved, far from any podium—Eric kept organizing games for the children and sharing hope with everyone around him. He ran his whole life with his eyes fixed on something beyond the finish line.

That's what it looks like when "Follow Me" gets all the way inside you. When Jesus isn't just a piece of your life but the center from which everything else flows. When surrender isn't a burden but a freedom.

The Restlessness You Feel Is an Invitation

Over sixteen hundred years ago, a young man in North Africa was brilliant, ambitious, and miserable. He'd tried everything his world offered—philosophy, career advancement, relationships—and came up empty every time. His mother, Monica, had prayed for his conversion for decades, but he kept running.

Then one day in a garden in Milan, Augustine finally stopped running. He described that moment and all the years leading to it in one of history's most famous prayers: "You have made us for yourself, O Lord, and our hearts are restless until they rest in you."

That restlessness Augustine described—you may be feeling it right now. The nagging sense that there must be more to faith than what you've experienced. The suspicion that the Christian life is supposed to be more transformative than your current version. The quiet hunger for something deeper, something truer, something that actually satisfies.

I want you to know: that restlessness isn't a problem. It's an invitation.

God put that holy discontent in you on purpose. It's His way of saying, "There's more. So much more. Will you come and find it?"

The same Jesus who walked the shoreline calling fishermen to follow is walking toward you right now. He's not disappointed in where you've been. He's not angry about what you haven't done. He's extending the same invitation He's been extending for two thousand years.

Follow Me.

Not "believe in Me" (though that's included). Not "agree with Me" (though that matters). Not "add Me to your busy life when you have time."

Follow Me.

Leave what you're holding. Step into something new. Discover the life you were actually created to live.

Are you ready to answer?

Study Guide: Introduction

Personal Reflection Questions

Take time alone with these questions. Be honest. No one is grading you—this is between you and God.

When you hear the phrase "cultural Christianity," what images or experiences come to mind? Do any of them describe your own faith journey?

Describe a moment when you sensed God might be calling you to something more—a deeper faith, a bigger purpose, a bolder step. What did you do with that prompting?

Peter, Andrew, James, and John left everything to follow Jesus. If Jesus called you to leave your "nets" today, what would be hardest for you to walk away from? Be specific.

Eric Liddell said he felt God's pleasure when he ran. What activities or moments make you feel God's pleasure in your life? When do you feel most fully alive in your faith?

Augustine wrote that our hearts are restless until they rest in God. Where do you feel restlessness in your spiritual life right now? What might God be saying to you through that restlessness?

Group Discussion Questions

For small groups, Sunday school classes, or discussion with a trusted friend.

How would you describe the difference between "believing in Jesus" and "following Jesus"? Why do you think many churches have emphasized one over the other?

Bonhoeffer warned about "cheap grace." In what ways do you see this playing out in American Christianity today? How do we guard against it without becoming legalistic or joyless?

Read John 10:10 together. What does "life to the full" mean to you? How is that different from the "abundant life" often marketed in prosperity gospel messages?

Think about the Old Testament figures mentioned—Abraham, Moses, Ruth, David. What common threads do you see in their stories? What made them willing to take such extraordinary risks?

As a group, discuss honestly: What would change in your church community if every member moved from cultural Christianity to surrendered discipleship? Dream big—what might become possible?

Action Step

This week, set aside fifteen minutes each day in silence and solitude. Find a place where you won't be interrupted—early morning, lunch break, after the kids go to bed, wherever works for you.

In that silence, ask God one simple question: "Lord, what more do You have for me?"

Don't rush to fill the silence. Don't check your phone. Just listen.

Keep a journal nearby and write down anything that comes to mind—thoughts, impressions, Scripture verses, ideas. Don't edit or judge what surfaces. Just capture it. At the end of the week, look back over what you've written. What patterns do you notice? What might God be saying?

"Follow Me."
— *Jesus of Nazareth*

CHAPTER ONE

THE WAKE-UP CALL

Recognizing the Difference Between Religion and Relationship

He came at night.

Of all the details John recorded about this encounter, that one has always fascinated me. Nicodemus didn't schedule a daytime appointment. He didn't show up at a public teaching session where others could see him engaging with Jesus. He waited until the streets of Jerusalem were empty, until the darkness could hide his curiosity, and then he made his way to wherever Jesus was staying.

Why the secrecy? Because Nicodemus had everything to lose.

This wasn't some spiritual seeker on the fringes of society. Nicodemus was a Pharisee—one of the religious elite. He was a member of the Sanhedrin, the ruling council of Israel. Think of him as a combination of a Supreme Court justice and a seminary president. If there was anyone in first-century Judaism who had religion figured out, it was Nicodemus. He knew the Torah (the Old Testament) backwards and forwards. He tithed with precision. He kept the Sabbath meticulously. He had the respect of his peers and the admiration of the people.

By every religious metric, Nicodemus was succeeding.

And yet.

Something drew him through those dark streets to find Jesus. Something whispered that all his religious accomplishment wasn't quite enough. He had mastered the system—and the system had left him empty. He could quote Scripture with the best of them, but somewhere deep in his soul, a question gnawed at him: "Is this all there is?"

I've met SO many Nicodemuses in my years of ministry. They don't usually come at night anymore—they catch me after a service, or send me an email or a text, or ask if we can grab coffee sometime. But that same look is in their eyes. That same unspoken question hangs in the air between us.

"I've gone to church my whole life. I've done all the right things. But something's missing. I don't know what it is, but I know it's missing."

If you've ever felt that way, this chapter is for you. Not to make you feel guilty—but because you can't get somewhere new until you honestly acknowledge where you're starting from. Before we can talk about the abundant life Jesus offers, we need to name the settled-for life so many of us are living.

Nicodemus represents every person who has checked all the religious boxes but still feels something essential is missing. The good news is that Jesus didn't turn him away. He engaged him. He offered him something he'd never found in all his religious striving.

He can do the same for you.

Seven Signs You Might Be Stuck in Cultural Christianity

I want to share with you seven warning signs—not to condemn, but to illuminate. As you read through these, I'd encourage you to ask the Holy Spirit to show you where you might be settling for religion instead of relationship. This isn't about being perfect; it's about being honest.

Faith by Geography

"I'm a Christian because I was born in America." Or, "I'm a Christian because my parents raised me in church."

I hear variations of this all the time, and I understand the sentiment. Many of us grew up in homes where faith was part of the family identity, as assumed as our last name. We went to church on Sundays like we went to school on weekdays—it was just what our family did. Some of you might be like me – I can track my family back through many generations and each was connected to churches in their communities. I even have a church that bears my family name.

But here's the thing: faith isn't inherited like eye color. You don't become a Christian by osmosis, absorbing it from the cultural water you swim in. If you'd been born in Saudi Arabia, you'd likely have grown up Muslim. If you'd been born in India, you'd probably identify as Hindu. Being born in the Bible Belt doesn't make you a disciple any more than being born in a garage makes you a car.

At some point, faith has to become your own. Not your parents' faith. Not your culture's faith. Yours. A conscious choice to follow Jesus, made with your own will, based on your own conviction.

Nicodemus was born into Jewish faith. He had ancestry stretching back to Abraham. But Jesus told him something shocking: "You must be born again." All that heritage meant nothing without personal transformation.

Compartmentalized Belief

This is one of the most common symptoms I see: Jesus gets Sunday morning, but Monday through Saturday operate by different rules.

We worship on the weekend and worry all week. We sing about trusting God and then lose sleep over our finances. We hear sermons about loving our enemies and then spend the afternoon complaining about our coworkers. We say "amen" to generosity in the sanctuary and pinch pennies in the marketplace.

Somehow, we've convinced ourselves that faith belongs in a box labeled "spiritual life"—neatly separated from our work life, our financial life, our family life, our recreational life. We let Jesus into the church building but post a "No Entry" sign on the rest of our existence.

The problem is, Jesus never agreed to those terms. When He said, "Follow Me," He wasn't talking about Sundays from 8:30 to noon. He was claiming Lordship over every square inch of our lives. Every decision. Every dollar. Every relationship. Every ambition. Either Jesus is Lord of all, or He isn't really Lord at all.

What would it look like if your faith showed up at the office on Monday? If it shaped how you handled that difficult conversation with your spouse? If it influenced what you watched, what you bought, how you voted?

Consumer Christianity

We live in a consumer culture, and it has infected our approach to church more than most of us realize.

Consumer Christianity evaluates church by what it offers me. Does the music fit my preferences? Is the preaching engaging enough to hold my attention? Are the facilities nice? Is there a good children's program for my kids? Is the parking convenient? Does the service fit my schedule?

Now, these aren't bad questions in themselves. Churches should strive for excellence, and it's legitimate to consider practical factors when choosing a church home. But when these become the primary criteria—when we approach church like we approach choosing a restaurant or a streaming service—something has gone wrong.

The question of consumer Christianity is always, "What can this church do for me?" The question of discipleship is, "What can I offer God and others through this community?"

When the early church gathered, they didn't evaluate the worship experience like critics reviewing a concert. They devoted themselves to teaching, fellowship, breaking bread, and prayer. They asked what they could contribute, not what they could consume. They understood that the church isn't a vendor of religious goods and services—it's a family, a body, a people on mission together.

A disciple asks: "Where am I needed? How can I serve? What can I give?" A consumer asks: "Where am I fed? How can I be served? What can I get?"

Moralistic Therapeutic Deism

A few years back, sociologists studying American religious beliefs coined a phrase that perfectly captures what many people actually believe, even if they'd never articulate it this way: Moralistic Therapeutic Deism.

It goes something like this: God exists. God wants people to be good, nice, and fair to each other. The central goal of life is to be happy and feel good about yourself. God doesn't need to be particularly involved in your life except when you have a problem—then He's like a cosmic emergency hotline, available when needed but otherwise staying in the background. And good people go to heaven when they die.

Sound familiar?

There are many people who say that this is the default religion of America—a vague belief in a distant God who exists primarily to make us happy and solve our problems. It's Christianity with all the inconvenient parts removed. No cross. No surrender. No transformation. No demands.

But here's what this sanitized version misses: God isn't a divine vending machine or a cosmic genie in a lamp, and the gospel isn't a self-help program with spiritual language. The God of Scripture is holy, intimate, demanding, and gracious. He doesn't exist for our agendas—He invites us into His. He doesn't just want us to be nice—He wants to make us new.

When Nicodemus came to Jesus, he probably expected a theological discussion between two teachers. Jesus told him he needed to be completely remade. That's not therapeutic—that's revolutionary.

Checking-the-Box Faith

This one hits close to home for a lot of church folks, including me if I'm honest.

Checking-the-box faith measures faithfulness by attendance. I showed up on some Sundays—check. I've been baptized—check. I put something in the offering plate—check. I served on a committee or on a mission project once—check. I attend the Christmas Eve and Easter services—check. I've done my part.

The boxes can even get more elaborate: I read my Bible every day (or at least most days). I say grace before many meals. I have been known to listen to Christian music. I have a fish emblem on my car. I don't curse (much). I'm basically a good person.

Check, check, check.

But here's the question nobody likes to ask: Is God impressed with your checklist? Is He keeping a tally somewhere, nodding approvingly as you rack up religious activities? God didn't gamify faith – where when we check enough boxes we get to level up.

The prophet Samuel told King Saul something worth remembering: "Does the Lord delight in burnt offerings and sacrifices as much as in obeying the Lord?" The answer, of course, is no. God isn't after our religious performance. He's after our hearts.

I've known people who could check every box on the Christian checklist, but who have spent decades angry at the world. People who never missed a Sunday but also never forgave a friend. People who tithed precisely but wouldn't give a struggling neighbor the time of day. The boxes were checked; the heart was untouched.

Discipleship isn't a checklist—it's a relationship. And relationships can't be reduced to tasks completed.

Risk-Free Religion

Here's a diagnostic question that cuts to the chase: When was the last time your faith required you to do something that scared you or really challenged you or at least made you stretch beyond your normal comfort zone?

If you can't remember, you might be practicing risk-free religion.

Risk-free religion keeps faith comfortable, predictable, and safe. It never asks you to have that hard conversation, give more than is comfortable, love someone who's difficult, or step out when you can't see the bottom. It's faith with all the adventure removed.

Think about the people in Scripture who actually followed God. Abraham left everything familiar for a destination he didn't know. Moses confronted Pharaoh with nothing but a staff and a stuttering tongue. David faced Goliath while grown warriors cowered. Esther risked death to speak up for her people. Peter stepped out of a boat onto waves.

Show me a biblical hero, and I'll show you someone who took risks for God.

Faith that requires no courage isn't faith at all—it's just routine. Real faith has an element of "this might not work" to it. Real faith steps out before all the answers are in. Real faith trusts God enough to look foolish, to fail, to sacrifice.

I think of the servants at the wedding in Cana. Jesus told them to fill stone jars with water, then draw some out and take it to the master of the banquet. They had no idea the water had become wine. Imagine the walk across that room, holding a ladle of what you're pretty sure is still just water, about to serve it to the most important person at the party.

That's what faith looks like. Obedient action before the miracle is visible.

Private Faith

"My faith is personal."

I hear this phrase a lot, and I understand what people usually mean by it. Faith is intimate. It involves the deepest parts of who we are. It's not something to be paraded around for show.

But sometimes "my faith is personal" is code for "my faith is invisible." It sounds spiritual, but what it really means is: "No one in my daily life would know I'm a Christian unless I told them."

Your coworkers don't see it. Your neighbors don't notice it. Your extended family can't point to any evidence of it. Your social media reflects every interest and opinion except your faith. If someone followed you around for a week without hearing you say the word "Christian," would they have any idea you belonged to Jesus?

Jesus said something uncomfortable about this: "Whoever is ashamed of me and my words, the Son of Man will be ashamed of them when he comes in his glory." That's not a threat—it's a warning. If we hide our connection to Jesus in this life, we shouldn't be surprised if that connection looks tenuous in the next.

Faith that's genuinely transforming has a way of showing up. It affects how we speak, how we treat people, what we prioritize. It leaks out. It creates curiosity. It makes people ask questions.

Remember Nicodemus, who came at night? He's an interesting study. At first, he was a secret inquirer, hiding his interest. But later in John's Gospel, we see him defending Jesus before the Sanhedrin. And after the crucifixion, he helped Joseph of Arimathea bury Jesus—a very public act that probably ended his career. Something happened between that first nighttime visit and the cross. It seems that his private faith became visible.

Faith may start in private, but it can't stay there.

When Religion Breaks God's Heart: A Warning from Hosea

If you think this struggle between religion and relationship is a modern problem, you haven't spent much time in the Old Testament prophets.

God's people in ancient Israel had the same tendency we do—turning faith into ritual, going through the motions while their hearts drifted elsewhere. They checked the boxes of their day: sacrifices at the temple, observance of feast days, payment of tithes. They were religious. They just weren't close to God.

Listen to the heartbreak in God's voice through the prophet Hosea:

"What can I do with you, Ephraim? What can I do with you, Judah? Your love is like the morning mist, like the early dew that disappears... For I desire mercy, not sacrifice, and acknowledgment of God rather than burnt offerings." —Hosea 6:4-6

Do you hear the pain in that? "What can I do with you?" This is God—the Creator of the universe, the One who needs nothing—and He sounds almost helpless. Not because He lacks power, but because He wants their hearts, not their habits. And their hearts keep evaporating like morning dew.

They had sacrifices down to a science. They knew exactly which animals to bring, which rituals to perform, which words to say. But God says that's not what He's looking for. He wants mercy, not sacrifice. He wants relationship, not religion. He wants them to actually know Him, not just know about Him.

The Hebrew word Hosea uses for "acknowledgment" is the same word used for the intimate knowledge between a husband and wife. That's what God is after—not formal, distant religion but intimate, knowing relationship.

You can fulfill every religious obligation and still miss the point entirely. Israel proved it. And so can we.

Jesus' Harshest Words Weren't for Sinners

Here's something that should make religious people like us squirm: Jesus saved His harshest criticism not for the obvious sinners but for the religious elite.

When Jesus encountered prostitutes, tax collectors, and adulterers, His tone was compassionate. "Neither do I condemn you. Go and sin no more." But when He encountered the Pharisees—the people who looked very religious, who tithed their spices and kept the minutiae of the law—His words were scorching.

In Matthew 23, Jesus unloaded on the religious leaders with a series of statements that must have made the crowd gasp. He called them blind guides, whitewashed tombs, snakes, a brood of vipers. He said they cleaned the outside of the cup while the inside was full of greed and self-indulgence. He said they traveled over land and sea to win a convert and then made that convert twice as much a child of hell as they were.

That's strong language. And Jesus wasn't having a bad day—He was making a point.

The religious leaders had built an entire system that kept people from actually knowing God. They had taken the living faith of Abraham, Moses, and David and turned it into a performance, a checklist, a burden. They had become experts in appearing righteous while their hearts were far from God.

And here's what breaks my heart: they didn't see it. They genuinely believed they were God's most faithful servants. They studied Scripture more than anyone, prayed longer than anyone, tithed more precisely than anyone. And they completely missed the God that Scripture, prayer, and tithing were supposed to lead them to.

Jesus' anger wasn't cruelty—it was grief. He looked at these religious professionals and saw people who had traded the real thing for a convincing counterfeit. And He loved them too much to let them keep sleepwalking toward destruction.

I wonder sometimes what Jesus would say to the church today. I wonder what He would say to me.

The Good News: It's Not Too Late

If you've recognized yourself in any of the descriptions above, please hear this: the point of this chapter is not to pile on guilt. We've got enough of that already.

The point is hope. Because here's the beautiful truth—the very fact that you're reading this book, the very fact that something in you resonates with these words, suggests that God is already at work in your heart. That holy restlessness isn't a sign that something's wrong with you. It's a sign that something's right.

God is calling you to more.

Remember Nicodemus? He came to Jesus at night, full of questions and confusion. He didn't fully understand what Jesus was saying about being born again—he even asked how a grown person could enter their mother's womb a second time. He shared his questions – he stayed engaged.

The Bible does give us the two additional glimpses of Nicodemus, and they tell a powerful story. In John 7, when the other Pharisees want to arrest Jesus, Nicodemus speaks up: "Does our law condemn a man without first hearing him?" It's not a bold confession of faith, but it's something. The seed Jesus planted is starting to sprout.

Then comes the clincher. After Jesus is crucified—after all the disciples except John have fled, after it looks like the whole movement has collapsed—Nicodemus shows up at the cross with Joseph of Arimathea. He brings seventy-five pounds of burial spices, an extravagant amount fit for a king. And together, they take Jesus' broken body and give it an honorable burial.

The man who came in secret at the beginning went public at the end—precisely when it was most dangerous to do so.

That's what happens when religion becomes relationship. That's what transformation looks like. Nicodemus started as a religious expert who had everything figured out. He ended as a disciple who risked everything for Jesus.

The same journey is available to you.

"Wake up, sleeper, rise from the dead, and Christ will shine on you."
—*Ephesians 5:14*

That verse was probably part of an early Christian hymn, sung to people who needed to wake from spiritual slumber. Maybe it's being sung over you right now. The question is whether you'll hit the snooze button or throw off the covers.

The Reluctant Convert: C.S. Lewis's Journey

I want to tell you about another man who had everything figured out—and discovered he was wrong.

Clive Staples Lewis—Jack to his friends—was a brilliant young scholar at Oxford in the 1920s. He was an atheist, and a smug one at that. He had rejected the Christianity of his childhood as so much superstitious nonsense, unworthy of an educated mind. The universe was matter and nothing more. When you died, you simply ceased to exist. And Lewis was quite content with this bleak conclusion.

At least, he thought he was.

Looking back on this period of his life, Lewis described himself as someone who, after a long sleep, still lies in bed, unwilling to face the cold. He knew something was wrong—he felt it in his restless pursuit of pleasure, in the unexpected joy that sometimes ambushed him through poetry or nature or memory. But he didn't want to get up. He didn't want to face what getting up might require.

What Lewis couldn't escape was a nagging sense that the universe made more sense if God existed than if He didn't. The materialist philosophy he'd embraced couldn't account for the things that mattered most to him—beauty, reason, morality, love. His atheism was intellectually satisfying in some ways, but it left him existentially homeless.

Then he started making dangerous friends. Brilliant men who were also committed Christians—men like J.R.R. Tolkien, who would later write The Lord of the Rings. These men challenged Lewis's assumptions, showed him that Christianity wasn't for intellectual lightweights, and lived out a faith that was both rigorous and real.

God was closing in, and Lewis knew it.

In his spiritual autobiography, Lewis described his conversion with characteristic honesty. He wrote that in the Trinity Term of 1929, he gave in and admitted that God was God, and knelt and prayed—perhaps that night, as he put it, he was the most dejected and reluctant convert in all England. He had not been seeking God; God had been seeking him, and he had run out of places to hide.

That night didn't make Lewis feel better—it made him feel cornered. But it was the beginning of everything. From that reluctant surrender would come some of the most influential Christian writing of the twentieth century. The Screwtape Letters. Mere Christianity. The Chronicles of Narnia. Books that have introduced millions to the faith Lewis once rejected.

What strikes me about Lewis's story is his honesty about the process. He didn't have a dramatic emotional experience. He didn't see visions or hear voices. He simply, finally, stopped running. He let go of his objections, his pride, his insistence on being in control. He admitted that the Hound of Heaven had caught him.

Maybe you're in that season right now. You've been running—from God, from commitment, from surrender. You've found comfortable places to hide, sophisticated reasons to resist. But God keeps pursuing. He keeps showing up in unexpected places. He keeps disturbing your settled unbelief.

What Lewis discovered is what everyone eventually discovers: you can surrender to God now, or you can surrender later, but you will surrender. The only question is how much of your life you'll waste fighting first.

An Invitation, Not a Condemnation

Let me be clear about something as we close this chapter: the goal isn't shame. I'm not trying to beat you up for being a cultural Christian—I've struggled with every symptom on that list myself. Religious habit comes naturally to me. Transformation takes effort.

The goal is hope. The goal is to help you see that the divine discontent you may be feeling is actually an invitation.

God isn't pointing a finger at you and saying, "Why haven't you done better?" He's extending a hand and saying, "There's so much more. Will you come?"

The religious boxes you've been checking - they were never meant to be the destination—they were supposed to be on-ramps to something deeper. The church attendance, the Bible reading, the moral effort—these are all good things, but they're not the point. The point is Jesus. The point is knowing Him, loving Him, following Him, becoming like Him.

And that kind of faith transforms everything.

Nicodemus started his journey confused and cautious. He ended it at the foot of a cross, going public with his allegiance to a crucified rabbi. That's transformation. That's what happens when religion becomes relationship.

C.S. Lewis started his journey running from God. He ended it using his brilliant mind in service of the kingdom. That's transformation. That's what happens when surrender replaces resistance.

The same story can be yours.

I don't know where you are as you read these words. Maybe you've been going through the motions for years, and this chapter has put language to what you've been feeling. Maybe you're angry at what I've written, which sometimes means it's hitting closer to home than you'd like to admit. Maybe you're cautiously hopeful that something more is actually available.

Wherever you are, I want you to know - God is patient with you. He's not tapping His foot, waiting for you to get your act together. He's inviting you—just as you are, with all your inconsistencies and failures—to something better.

The wake-up call is sounding. Will you open your eyes?

Study Guide: Chapter One

Personal Reflection Questions

Take time alone with these questions. Be honest. This is between you and God.

Review the "Seven Signs of Cultural Christianity." Which ones, if any, do you recognize in your own life? Don't rush past this question—sit with it. Ask the Holy Spirit to show you your blind spots.

Nicodemus came to Jesus at night, perhaps because he was afraid of what others might think. What fears have kept you from going deeper with Jesus? What are you afraid people might think or say?

If someone followed you around for a week without hearing you say you're a Christian, would they be able to tell? What evidence would they see? What would be missing?

God told Israel through Hosea, "I desire mercy, not sacrifice." What "sacrifices" (church activities, religious duties, moral efforts) might you be offering God instead of your heart?

C.S. Lewis described being "unwilling to get up and face the cold." What comfort zone is God asking you to leave? What would "getting up" look like for you right now?

Group Discussion Questions

For small groups, Sunday school classes, or discussion with a trusted friend.

Why do you think cultural Christianity is so prevalent in America? What cultural factors have contributed to this? What role has the church itself played?

Read John 3:1-21 together. What stands out to you about Jesus's conversation with Nicodemus? Why do you think Nicodemus struggled to understand what Jesus was saying? What would "being born again" have meant to a Pharisee?

Discuss the concept of "Moralistic Therapeutic Deism"—the idea that God exists mainly to make us happy and solve our problems. Have you encountered this view of God? How does it differ from biblical Christianity?

How can a church help people move from cultural Christianity to authentic discipleship without creating legalism or judgment? What would that look like practically?

Share a time when you experienced a spiritual "wake-up call." What prompted it? How did it change you? If you haven't had one yet, what do you sense God might be stirring in you now?

Action Step

This week, ask three people who know you well—a family member, a coworker, and a friend—this simple question: "What would you say is most important to me?"

Don't explain why you're asking. Don't defend yourself. Just listen.

Write down their answers. Then spend time in prayer asking God to show you: Does my life reflect what I say matters most? Is my faith visible, or is it hidden? What needs to change?

This exercise takes courage, but it will show you how your faith appears to those around you—which may be very different from how it feels on the inside.

"You must be born again."
— *Jesus to Nicodemus*

CHAPTER TWO

COUNTING THE COST

What Jesus Actually Asks of His Followers

He looked at the crowd and decided to thin the herd.

That's not how we usually tell the story of Jesus, is it? We prefer the parts where Jesus welcomes everyone, embraces the outcasts, and offers unconditional acceptance. And all of that is true. But there's another side to Jesus that makes us squirm—the side that looks at enthusiastic followers and essentially says, "Are you sure you know what you're signing up for?"

Luke's Gospel tells us that "large crowds were traveling with Jesus" (Luke 14:25, NIV). That's the kind of line that would make any pastor's heart sing. The movement is growing! The message is spreading! People are showing up!

But watch what Jesus does next. Instead of congratulating Himself on the impressive turnout, He stops, turns to face the crowd, and delivers one of the most jarring statements in all of Scripture:

"If anyone comes to me and does not hate father and mother, wife and children, brothers and sisters—yes, even their own life—such a person cannot be my disciple. And whoever does not carry their cross and follow me cannot be my disciple." —Luke 14:26-27 (NIV)

Hate your family? Carry your cross? This isn't exactly the seeker-friendly message we've been trained to deliver. Jesus sounds like He's actively trying to discourage people from following Him.

And in a sense, He is.

Jesus wasn't interested in enthusiastic beginners who would quit when things got hard. He wasn't looking for crowds—He was looking for disciples. And there's a profound difference between someone who shows up for the excitement and someone who has counted the cost and decided Jesus is worth whatever it takes.

To drive the point home, Jesus tells two mini-parables right there on the roadside. First, He describes a man who starts building a tower without calculating whether he can finish it—and ends up the laughingstock of the town when his money runs out and the foundation sits there abandoned. Then He pictures a king going to war who doesn't first consider whether his ten thousand troops can defeat an army of twenty thousand. If not, he'd better send a peace delegation while the enemy is still far away.

The message is unmistakable: before you sign on, know what you're signing on for. Discipleship isn't a free trial you can cancel when it gets inconvenient. It's not a membership with no commitment. Jesus wants informed followers who have looked at the price tag and said, "Yes, I'm in—whatever it costs."

Then comes the summary statement that should make all of us pause:

"In the same way, those of you who do not give up everything you have cannot be my disciples." —Luke 14:33 (NIV)

Everything. Not most things. Not the things we weren't using anyway. Everything.

This chapter isn't meant to scare you away from following Jesus. It's meant to prepare you for what following Him actually means. Because here's what I've learned in thirty-five years of ministry: people who understand the cost upfront don't get blindsided when discipleship gets hard. They expected hard. They signed up for it.

So, let's do what Jesus invited that crowd to do. Let's count the cost.

What Jesus Actually Asks

When I read the Gospels carefully, I find at least three non-negotiable demands Jesus places on anyone who wants to be His disciple. They're not suggestions. They're not for the super-spiritual. They're the baseline requirements for following Jesus.

Reordered Priorities

"If anyone comes to me and does not hate father and mother, wife and children, brothers and sisters—yes, even their own life—such a person cannot be my disciple."

Let's address that "hate" word immediately, because it sounds like Jesus is contradicting everything else He taught about love.

In the ancient Jewish world, "hate" was often used as a comparative term, not an emotional one. It didn't mean harboring animosity—it meant prioritizing one thing over another so decisively that the lesser thing looked like rejection by comparison. When Malachi reports God saying "Jacob I loved, but Esau I hated" (Malachi 1:2-3), God wasn't expressing disgust toward Esau. He was expressing His choice of Jacob's line for a particular purpose.

So, what is Jesus saying? He's saying that your love for Him must be so supreme, so all-encompassing, so absolute, that every other relationship—even the most precious ones—looks pale by comparison. Your devotion to Jesus must be so complete that people notice that He's your favorite, your preferred, your priority.

This isn't about neglecting your family or treating them poorly. Jesus condemned the Pharisees for using religious vows to avoid caring for their parents. He cares deeply about family. But He's making clear that no relationship, no matter how intimate, can compete with your allegiance to Him.

In practice, this means that when following Jesus conflicts with family expectations, Jesus wins. When your relative wants you to compromise your integrity, Jesus wins. When your career advancement requires you to set aside your convictions, Jesus wins. When your friends want you to go somewhere your conscience says no, Jesus wins.

Every relationship. Every ambition. Every comfort. Every security. All of it gets rearranged around one central loyalty: Jesus is Lord.

Notice He even includes "their own life." Not just the people you love—but you. Your preferences. Your plans. Your self-interest. All of it bows to Jesus, if you want to be His disciple.

That's what He said.

Daily Cross-Bearing

"Whoever does not carry their cross and follow me cannot be my disciple."

We've softened this phrase into meaninglessness. We talk about difficult situations—a frustrating job, a chronic illness, a challenging family member—as "my cross to bear." It's become a synonym for inconvenience.

But that's not what the cross meant to Jesus's original hearers.

The cross was a Roman instrument of execution. It was reserved for the worst criminals and was designed to maximize both suffering and humiliation. Victims were sometimes forced to carry the crossbeam through the streets to their place of death—a final public shaming before the end came.

When Jesus told the crowd to "carry their cross," He wasn't talking about putting up with difficult circumstances. He was talking about dying. He was saying: "Follow me to your death. Die to your old self. Die to your old priorities. Die to the life you thought you were going to live."

The apostle Paul understood this. He wrote to the Galatians, "I have been crucified with Christ and I no longer live, but Christ lives in me" (Galatians 2:20, NIV). That's not poetry—that's the job description. The old Paul was dead. A new creation had taken his place.

Luke's Gospel adds a detail the other writers don't include. In Luke 9:23, Jesus says we must take up our cross "daily." Not once for all. Not at a dramatic altar call that we look back on for the rest of our lives. Every single day.

Every morning, the disciple wakes up and dies again. Dies to self-will. Dies to self-promotion. Dies to the cultural values that constantly whisper, "Look out for number one." Every day is a new opportunity to say, "Not my will, but Yours be done."

This is the part of discipleship nobody puts on the brochure. But Jesus put it at the front of His invitation. He wanted people to know: this will cost you your life. Not someday. Not if things go badly. Every day.

Total Surrender

"Those of you who do not give up everything you have cannot be my disciples."

Everything you have. Not just the stuff you don't need anymore. Not just the money you can spare after you've paid your bills. Everything.

Now, before you panic, let me explain what I think Jesus means—and doesn't mean—by this.

Jesus isn't saying that every disciple must literally sell everything and live in poverty. We know this because not everyone in the Gospels who followed Jesus divested all their assets. Joseph of Arimathea was wealthy and used his resources to bury Jesus. Lydia in Acts was a successful businesswoman who supported Paul's ministry. The issue isn't possession—it's ownership.

Here's the distinction: a disciple holds everything with open hands. Nothing is truly "mine" anymore—it's all on loan from God, to be used for His purposes. My house is His house. My car is His car. My resources are His resources. My time is His time. My talents are His talents.

The opposite of surrender is grasping, hoarding, clutching—holding onto things so tightly that God would have to pry them from your fingers. A surrendered disciple has learned to let go before being asked. Not because stuff is bad, but because stuff is never allowed to compete with Jesus.

I think of the rich young ruler, whom we'll discuss shortly. His problem wasn't that he was wealthy. His problem was that his wealth had a grip on his heart that he wasn't willing to break. When Jesus asked him to release it, he couldn't. The stuff had become his master, even though he thought he was the one in control.

Total surrender means Jesus is Lord of all—your calendar, your checkbook, your relationships, your future, your reputation. Everything is on the table. Nothing is held back. You've signed over the title to your whole life.

Abraham: The Original Cost-Counter

If you want to see what counting the cost looks like in real life, look at Abraham.

The story begins in Genesis 12, when Abraham (still called Abram at this point) was living a comfortable life in Ur of the Chaldeans. He had family, security, a place in the community. Then God spoke:

"Go from your country, your people and your father's household to the land I will show you." —Genesis 12:1 (NIV)

Notice what God told Abraham and what He didn't.

God told him to leave. That was clear. Leave your country—the only land you've ever known. Leave your people—your cultural identity, your connections, your support system. Leave your father's household—the family business, your inheritance, the people who would care for you in old age.

But God didn't tell Abraham where he was going. "The land I will show you"—that's it. No map. No GPS coordinates. No brochure with pictures of the destination. Just a command to leave everything familiar and start walking.

Can you imagine that conversation with his wife Sarah? "Honey, I've got news. We're moving." "Oh? Where?" "I don't know yet." "What do you mean you don't know?" "God will show us when we get there." "When we get where?"

By every reasonable calculation, this made no sense. Abraham was seventy-five years old—not exactly the age to start over somewhere new. He had no children to carry on his legacy if things went wrong. He was being asked to trade security for uncertainty, the known for the unknown, a predictable future for a promise from a God he was just getting to know.

The cost was enormous. And Abraham counted it.

Then he went.

Genesis 12:4 is one of the most understated verses in the Bible: "So Abram went, as the Lord had told him." No recorded objection. No negotiation. No request for a trial period. He went.

That's what counting the cost produces. Not blind impulsiveness, but informed obedience. Abraham understood what he was giving up. He just decided that what God was offering was worth more.

But the cost-counting wasn't over. Years later, after God had miraculously provided the son He'd promised, the test came again. Genesis 22 records the moment when God asked Abraham to sacrifice Isaac—the child of promise, the heir through whom all the blessings were supposed to flow, the son Abraham had waited twenty-five years to hold.

"Take your son, your only son, whom you love—Isaac—and go to the region of Moriah. Sacrifice him there as a burnt offering." (Genesis 22:2, NIV)

I can barely type those words without feeling the weight of them. This wasn't a theoretical test. This was God asking Abraham to give up the thing he loved most in the world—the thing that represented all his hopes for the future, all God's promises come true.

And Abraham went. Early the next morning, he saddled his donkey, took Isaac, and headed for Moriah. He didn't argue. He didn't delay. He had already counted the cost once before, and he knew the answer: whatever God asks is worth it. Even this.

The book of Hebrews tells us what was going through Abraham's mind:

"Abraham reasoned that God could even raise the dead" (Hebrews 11:19, NIV). His faith had grown so strong through the first test that he trusted God even when the math made no sense. If God wanted Isaac dead, God could bring him back. The promise couldn't fail, even if Abraham couldn't see how.

Of course, God stopped Abraham's hand at the last moment. A ram appeared in the thicket, and Isaac was spared. But here's what I want you to see: Abraham didn't know that was coming. He climbed that mountain believing he was going to lose his son. He had counted the cost and decided that obedience to God was worth even that.

That's what disciples do. They count the cost. They decide Jesus is worth it. And they keep walking, even when they can't see how it's all going to work out.

The Surprising Exchange

Now here's where the economics of discipleship get strange.

Jesus asked His followers to give up everything. Reordered priorities. Daily cross. Total surrender. The cost is real, and I don't want to minimize it. Anyone who tells you discipleship is easy hasn't read the Gospels carefully.

But Jesus also made a promise that flips the entire equation upside down:

"Whoever wants to save their life will lose it, but whoever loses their life for me will find it." —Matthew 16:25 (NIV)

Read that again slowly. The person who clutches their life, who refuses to surrender, who holds back from full commitment—that person ends up losing the very thing they were trying to protect. But the person who lets go, who surrenders everything, who loses their life for Jesus's sake—that person finds something better than what they released.

This is the great paradox of the kingdom: you gain by giving up. You find by losing. You live by dying.

I've watched this play out in real lives over and over. The couple who gives generously discovers a joy that hoarders never experience. The career professional who risks reputation to stand for integrity gains a peace that climbers never find. The parent who releases a child to follow God's call receives a deeper relationship than control ever produced.

When we surrender everything, we don't end up with nothing. We end up with everything that matters.

Elisabeth Elliot understood this. Her husband Jim was one of the five missionaries killed in Ecuador in 1956 (we'll talk more about them shortly). She lost the person she loved most in the world to a spear thrust in the jungle. By any normal calculation, her life should have been defined by that loss.

Instead, Elisabeth went back. She returned to Ecuador, lived among the very people who had killed her husband, and spent years sharing the gospel with them. She could have been bitter. She could have walked away from faith entirely. Instead, she discovered something deeper than safety—a purpose that transcended her pain.

Years later, Elisabeth wrote about finding rest in God's will, describing it as immeasurably beyond anything she could have imagined or planned for herself. She had lost her husband, lost her plans, lost the life she thought she would have. And in the losing, she found something she never would have found otherwise.

That's the economy of the kingdom. The cost is real. But so is the return. And the return is always greater than what we gave up.

One of the great devotional writers of the twentieth century, A.W. Tozer, expressed it beautifully when he noted that the person who has God for their treasure possesses everything of value in one possession. When you have God, you have it all—because everything good comes from Him anyway. The things we're afraid to release are just shadows of the reality we gain when we let go.

The Rich Young Ruler: A Cautionary Tale

Not everyone who counts the cost decides to pay it.

Mark's Gospel tells us about a young man who did the math and walked away. His story is one of the saddest in Scripture—not because of what he did, but because of what he missed.

The encounter begins in a promising way. "As Jesus started on his way, a man ran up to him and fell on his knees before him" (Mark 10:17, NIV). This wasn't a casual seeker strolling by with a question. This man ran. He was eager, desperate even. And he knelt—a posture of humility and respect.

"Good teacher," he asked, "what must I do to inherit eternal life?"

It's a great question. The man sensed that something was missing despite all his religious achievement. He had kept the commandments since childhood—no murder, no adultery, no stealing, no lying, no fraud, honor your parents. By every measurable standard, he was a moral success.

But he knew it wasn't enough. Something gnawed at him, some holy restlessness that all his rule-keeping couldn't satisfy. That's why he ran to Jesus looking for the answer.

What happens next is remarkable. Mark tells us that "Jesus looked at him and loved him" (Mark 10:21, NIV). Before He said a word of challenge, Jesus loved this man. The demand that followed wasn't cruelty—it was surgery. Jesus was going to cut away the one thing keeping this man from abundant life.

"One thing you lack," Jesus said. "Go, sell everything you have and give to the poor, and you will have treasure in heaven. Then come, follow me."

Jesus saw what the man himself probably couldn't see: his wealth had become his god. Not money itself—money is neutral. But this man's relationship to his money had enslaved him. His possessions possessed him. The one thing standing between him and the life he was asking about was the one thing he wasn't willing to release.

The man's face fell. "He went away sad, because he had great wealth" (Mark 10:22, NIV).

He counted the cost. And he decided it was too high.

I want you to notice two things about this story.

First, Jesus let him go. He didn't chase after him. He didn't renegotiate the terms. He didn't say, "Okay, how about you just give two percent now and then over the rest of your life you can keep increasing percentages?" Jesus loved this man enough to tell him the truth, and He loved him enough to let him choose.

God will never force discipleship on anyone. He invites. He challenges. He tells us the truth about what it costs and what it offers. But He leaves the choice with us.

Second, notice how the man felt as he walked away. He didn't leave triumphant, celebrating his independence. He left sad. He knew he was giving up something precious. He just couldn't make himself let go.

That's the tragedy of refusing the call. It doesn't lead to freedom—it leads to sadness. The man kept his wealth but lost his joy. He preserved his comfort but forfeited his purpose. He held onto what he could count and missed what he couldn't measure.

I wonder sometimes what happened to that young man. Did he ever change his mind? Did he watch from a distance as the movement grew without him? Did he hear about the resurrection and realize what he'd missed? We don't know. The Gospels never mention him again.

But I know this: he made a choice that day that defined his life. And every one of us faces the same choice. Jesus is still looking at us with love and saying, "Here's what stands between you and the life you're looking for. Will you let it go?"

What's your "one thing"? What would Jesus put His finger on if He looked at you with love and told you the truth?

He Is No Fool: Jim Elliot and the Ecuador Five

I want to tell you about five young men who counted the cost, paid the price, and changed the world.

In January 1956, Jim Elliot, Nate Saint, Ed McCully, Pete Fleming, and Roger Youderian landed on a sandbar in the jungles of Ecuador. Their mission: make peaceful contact with the Huaorani people, one of the most violent tribes in the Amazon. The Huaorani had killed so many outsiders that neighboring tribes called them Aucas—"savages." No one had ever succeeded in reaching them with the gospel.

These five men knew the risk. They weren't naive idealists wandering into danger without counting the cost. They had spent months preparing, dropping gifts to the Huaorani from their small airplane, learning phrases in their language, praying for the opportunity to share Christ.

Jim Elliot, in particular, had spent years wrestling with what it meant to follow Jesus completely. As a college student at Wheaton, he had written words in his journal that would become famous: "He is no fool who gives what he cannot keep to gain that which he cannot lose."

Think about that for a moment. What Jim was saying is that everything we clutch so tightly—our money, our safety, our lives—we're going to lose eventually anyway. You can't take it with you. But what we give to God, what we invest in His kingdom, what we surrender for His purposes—that's the only thing that lasts forever.

Jim had counted the cost. He knew exactly what he might be giving up. And he had decided it was worth it.

On January 8, 1956, a group of Huaorani warriors attacked the five missionaries on that sandbar. All five were killed. Jim Elliot was twenty-eight years old.

If this story ended there, it would be a tragedy—five young lives cut short, five widows left behind, five families shattered. The world would have called it a waste.

But the story didn't end there.

Two years later, Jim's widow Elisabeth—along with Rachel Saint, Nate's sister—went back to live among the Huaorani. They moved into the village, learned the language, and over time, shared the love of Christ with the very people who had killed their loved ones.

The results were nothing short of miraculous. Many Huaorani came to faith, including some of the men who had participated in the killings. The tribe that had been known for violence became known for transformation. A warrior named Mincaye, who was among the killers, became a believer and a dear friend of Steve Saint, Nate's son. He helped raise Steve's children and spoke at churches around the world about the forgiveness that changed his life.

Years later, when people asked if the sacrifice had been worth it, the answer was written in changed lives, in a transformed community, in a gospel witness that reached around the globe. The five men who died on that sandbar accomplished more through their deaths than many of us will accomplish through our entire lives.

Because they had counted the cost.

They knew what they were risking. They went anyway. And the fruit of their obedience is still being harvested today.

I'm not suggesting that every disciple will be called to physical martyrdom. Most of us won't. But every disciple is called to the same underlying commitment: Jesus is worth whatever it costs. My life is not my own. I've been bought with a price, and I'm available for whatever God wants to do with me.

Jim Elliot wasn't a fool. Neither was Abraham. Neither was Paul, or Peter, or any of the countless believers throughout history who have paid the price of discipleship. They counted the cost. They saw something worth more than what they were giving up. And they said yes.

The Question Before You

Jesus isn't trying to scare you away from following Him. He's trying to prepare you for what following Him means.

A soldier who understands what combat is like fights differently than one who expects a parade. A mountain climber who respects the terrain prepares differently than a casual hiker. An investor who knows the risks makes better decisions than one chasing quick returns.

Jesus wants informed followers. He wants people who know what they're signing up for and choose Him anyway—not because they don't understand the cost, but because they've decided He's worth it.

So, here's the question this chapter puts before you: Have you counted the cost?

Not have you believed in Jesus—we covered that distinction in the introduction. But have you looked honestly at what following Him requires and said, "Yes, I'm in. Whatever it costs. Whatever you ask. Wherever you lead."

The cost is real. Reordered priorities. Daily cross-bearing. Total surrender. It will mean saying no to some things you want and yes to some things you'd rather avoid. It will mean being different from the people around you, misunderstood by some, rejected by others.

But the return is also real. A life of purpose instead of drift. Joy that circumstances can't steal. Peace that transcends understanding. The unshakeable knowledge that your life matters, that you're part of something eternal, that every day has significance because you're living for the only thing worth living for.

The rich young ruler walked away sad, clutching his wealth, missing the treasure. Don't be that person.

Abraham left everything familiar and discovered God's blessing on the other side. Jim Elliot gave his life on a jungle sandbar and gained what can never be lost. Elisabeth Elliot surrendered her grief and found purpose beyond her pain.

The same exchange is available to you.

What you give up, you were going to lose anyway. What you gain lasts forever.

Have you counted the cost?

Are you ready to pay it?

———————————

"Those of you who do not give up everything you have cannot be my disciples."
— *Jesus of Nazareth*

12

Study Guide: Chapter Two

Personal Reflection Questions

Take time alone with these questions. Be honest. This is between you and God.

What would be the hardest thing for you to surrender to God—a relationship, a dream, financial security, reputation, entitlement, comfort? Be specific. Don't give the "right" answer; give the honest one.

Jesus said we must "hate" family to follow Him. What do you think He meant? In practical terms, what would it look like for your love for Jesus to be so supreme that other loves look pale by comparison?

The rich young ruler went away sad. Have you ever walked away from something God asked you to do? What happened? How did it feel then—and how does it feel now looking back?

Jim Elliot wrote about giving what he cannot keep to gain what he cannot lose. What are you trying to "keep" that you cannot ultimately hold onto? What might you gain if you released it?

When you think about total surrender to God, what fears come up? Name them specifically. What would help you move past those fears?

Group Discussion Questions

For small groups, Sunday school classes, or discussion with a trusted friend.

Why do you think Jesus was so upfront about the cost of discipleship? How does this differ from how we often present the gospel today? What might change if we were more honest about the cost?

Read Mark 10:17-27 together. What do you think Jesus saw in this young man? Why did He love him (v. 21) but still let him walk away? What does this teach us about how God works with us?

Discuss the paradox: "Whoever loses their life for me will find it." How have you seen this play out in your own life or someone else's? Does this promise feel real to you, or does it sound too good to be true?

The widows of the Ecuador missionaries returned to the people who killed their husbands. What enabled them to do that? What does their story teach us about the nature of Christian surrender and the power of forgiveness?

How can we help each other count the cost without becoming discouraged or legalistic? What's the difference between healthy challenge and unhealthy burden?

Action Step

This week, take a blank piece of paper and write down the three things you would be most reluctant to surrender to God. Be specific. Not vague categories like "my future"—but concrete things: "My retirement savings." "My relationship with [name]." "My dream of [specific goal]." "My reputation at work."

Then spend time in prayer with each one. You don't have to give them up today—this isn't about dramatic gestures. It's about honesty.

Pray something like this: "Lord, I'm holding this tightly. I don't want to let go. But I don't want it to own me. Help me love you more. Help me to trust you more. Help me to hold this with open hands. Give me the willingness to be willing."

Keep that paper somewhere you'll see it. Return to those prayers throughout the week. Notice what shifts in your heart as you bring these things honestly before God.

The goal isn't to feel guilty. The goal is to begin the process of surrender—not in one dramatic moment, but in the daily, honest, sometimes difficult work of saying, "Jesus, You are Lord of this too."

13

CHAPTER THREE

THE SURRENDERED LIFE

Discovering Your Purpose Through Complete Yielding

She was just a teenager with a plan.

Mary thought she knew how her life would be lived out—or at least she knew as much as any young woman in first-century Nazareth could. She was engaged to Joseph, a respectable carpenter with a good trade and steady hands. In a few months, they'd be married. She'd move into his home, start a family, and settle into the rhythm that generations of women before her had followed. It wasn't glamorous, but it was good. Safe. Predictable.

Then an angel showed up and wrecked everything.

Luke's Gospel tells us that Gabriel appeared to Mary with news that would turn her entire existence upside down. She, a virgin, would conceive a child by the Holy Spirit. This child would be called the Son of the Most High and would reign on David's throne forever. The impossible was about to happen—in her body, through her life, at the cost of everything she had planned.

Try to imagine what went through Mary's mind in that moment. This wasn't just an inconvenience to her schedule. This was social ruin. In her culture, an unmarried pregnant woman faced disgrace, divorce, potentially even death by stoning. Joseph would have every right to walk away. Her family would be shamed. The life she had envisioned—the safe, predictable, respectable life—was about to vanish.

And yet.

Listen to her response: "I am the Lord's servant. May your word to me be fulfilled" (Luke 1:38, NIV).

No negotiation. No request for time to think it over. No list of concerns or conditions. Just surrender. Complete, breathtaking, terrifying surrender.

That moment in Nazareth captures something essential about what it means to follow God. Mary didn't fully understand what she was agreeing to. She couldn't have known that this baby would grow up to be rejected by His own people, tortured by Roman soldiers, and executed on a cross while she watched helplessly. She couldn't have foreseen the sword that would pierce her own soul, as the old prophet Simeon would later predict.

All she knew was that God was asking something of her—something costly, something confusing, something that would require letting go of the life she had imagined. And her answer was yes.

That's the essence of the surrendered life. Not understanding everything, but trusting anyway. Not seeing the whole path, but taking the next step. Not holding onto our plans with white knuckles, but opening our hands and saying, "Lord, I'm Yours. Whatever that means, wherever that leads, I'm Yours."

In the last chapter, we counted the cost of discipleship. We looked honestly at what Jesus asks of His followers—reordered priorities, daily cross-bearing, total surrender. If that chapter made you gulp, good. It should have. Jesus never soft-pedaled the demands of following Him.

But here's what I want you to see in this chapter: surrender isn't just about what you give up. It's about what you find. The surrendered life isn't the diminished life—it's the discovered life. When we stop clutching our plans and start opening our hands, something remarkable happens. We find the purpose we've been searching for all along.

What Surrender Actually Means (and Doesn't Mean)

Before we go any further, I need to clear up some misconceptions. The word "surrender" carries baggage for many people. It sounds like defeat. Like giving up. Like waving a white flag and admitting you've lost.

But biblical surrender is nothing like that. Let me show you what surrender is—and what it isn't.

Surrender Is Not Passivity

Some people hear "surrender to God" and picture sitting in a chair, hands folded, waiting for divine instructions to be delivered by celestial courier. Just check out of life and let God do whatever He's going to do.

That's not surrender—that's abdication. And it's the opposite of what Mary modeled.

After the angel left, Mary didn't sit around passively. She actively traveled to visit her cousin Elizabeth. She actively pondered the things that were happening to her. She actively raised Jesus through childhood, teaching Him the Scriptures, caring for His needs, shaping His early years. She actively followed His ministry, showing up at the cross when almost everyone else had fled, staying until the bitter end.

Surrender is not passive resignation. It's active cooperation with God's purposes. We don't just sit back and let life happen to us. We engage, we serve, we work, we love—but we do all of it with open hands, ready to adjust course whenever God redirects.

Think of it like a dance. In partner dancing, one person leads and the other follows. But the follower isn't passive—they're actively moving, responding, adjusting. They're fully engaged, just not trying to be in control. That's what surrender looks like. We're dancing with God, letting Him lead, but fully present and fully engaged in every step.

Surrender Is Not Losing Your Personality

Here's a fear I've encountered many times over the years: "If I surrender completely to God, I'll become some religious nut. I'll lose what makes me me."

I get it. The idea of surrender can feel like annihilation—like you're supposed to disappear into some generic "Christian" mold and come out the other side as a boring, colorless version of yourself.

But that's not what happens at all. God didn't make you to erase you. He made you because He wanted you—your specific personality, your unique gifts, your particular way of seeing the world. Surrender doesn't delete those things; it redeems them.

Look at the disciples. After surrendering to Jesus, Peter was still impulsive and bold. John was still thoughtful and deep. Matthew still had an eye for details. Thomas still asked hard questions. Their personalities weren't erased—they were sanctified, redirected, put to use for the kingdom.

When you surrender to God, you don't become less yourself. You become more yourself—the self you were always meant to be before sin distorted and diminished you. You become the person God had in mind when He formed you in your mother's womb.

Surrender Is Not Giving Up Your Dreams

"But what about my dreams? My goals? The things I've been working toward my whole life?"

Here's the paradox: surrender doesn't mean giving up your dreams. It means exchanging your dreams for God's dreams. And God's dreams for you are always—always—larger than what you could have imagined for yourself.

Think about Mary again. She probably dreamed of being a good wife to Joseph, raising children in a faithful home, living out her days in relative peace. Those weren't bad dreams. But God had something bigger in mind. She would become the most celebrated woman in human history, the mother of the Savior, blessed among all generations. Her name would be remembered and honored for two thousand years and counting.

She couldn't have dreamed that for herself. It was beyond her imagination. But it was exactly what God had planned.

When we surrender our dreams to God, we're not settling for less. We're making room for more. We're saying, "Lord, I had some ideas about what my life should look like. But Your ideas are better. Show me what You've got."

Surrender Is Not a One-Time Event

This might be the most important clarification of all. Surrender is not a single moment—it's a daily posture.

Yes, there may be a dramatic moment when you first say yes to Jesus, when you first release control and decide to follow wherever He leads. That moment matters. But it's just the beginning.

Every morning, we wake up with our hands curled around something—our plans, our preferences, our fears, our rights. Every morning, surrender means consciously opening those hands again. "Lord, today I choose You. Today I release my agenda and embrace Yours. Today, not my will but Yours be done."

This is what Jesus meant when He told us to take up our cross daily. Not once for all. Not at a summer camp experience we look back on fondly. Every single day.

Surrender is a posture we return to again and again, sometimes multiple times in a single day. It's a habit we cultivate, a muscle we strengthen, a direction we keep choosing even when everything in us wants to grab the wheel back.

When God Shows Up: Isaiah's Throne Room Encounter

If you want to understand how surrender actually happens, look at the prophet Isaiah.

In the sixth chapter of his book, Isaiah describes a vision that changed everything. "In the year that King Uzziah died," he writes, "I saw the Lord, high and exalted, seated on a throne; and the train of his robe filled the temple" (Isaiah 6:1, NIV).

The timing matters. King Uzziah had reigned for fifty-two years—virtually Isaiah's entire lifetime. His death represented the end of an era, a moment of national uncertainty. And it was in this moment of instability that Isaiah received a vision of the only throne that never wobbles.

What he saw was overwhelming. Seraphim—angelic beings—flew above the throne, calling out to one another: "Holy, holy, holy is the Lord Almighty; the whole earth is full of his glory" (Isaiah 6:3, NIV).

The doorposts shook. The temple filled with smoke. Isaiah had a front-row seat to the majesty of God.

And his response? It wasn't worship, at least not initially. It wasn't praise or excitement or joy.

It was terror.

"Woe to me!" Isaiah cried. "I am ruined! For I am a man of unclean lips, and I live among a people of unclean lips, and my eyes have seen the King, the Lord Almighty" (Isaiah 6:5, NIV).

This is what always happens when human beings get an unfiltered glimpse of God's holiness. We don't feel proud of our spiritual accomplishments. We don't congratulate ourselves on how far we've come. We see ourselves clearly—and what we see is devastating. Isaiah wasn't being melodramatic. He genuinely felt ruined, undone, exposed.

But here's the beautiful part. God didn't leave Isaiah in that state.

One of the seraphim flew to Isaiah with a live coal from the altar. He touched Isaiah's lips with it and said, "See, this has touched your lips; your guilt is taken away and your sin atoned for" (Isaiah 6:7, NIV).

Before God asked anything of Isaiah, He cleansed him. Before the commission came the forgiveness. Before "Go" came "You're forgiven." God meets us in our inadequacy, not after we've cleaned ourselves up but while we're still a mess.

And then—only then—came the invitation.

"Then I heard the voice of the Lord saying, 'Whom shall I send? And who will go for us?'" (Isaiah 6:8, NIV).

Notice that God didn't command. He asked. He was looking for a volunteer, not conscripting a soldier. The mission He had in mind required someone willing, not someone forced.

And Isaiah's response is the model for every surrendered disciple:

"Here am I. Send me!" (Isaiah 6:8, NIV).

Five words that changed a life and shaped a nation. (Like we said earlier about the disciples) Isaiah didn't ask for the job description first. He didn't negotiate terms or request time to think about it. He simply made himself available. "Here am I. Send me."

This is the pattern of surrender. It begins with a vision of who God is—His holiness, His majesty, His otherness. It continues with honesty about who we are—our inadequacy, our failure, our desperate need for grace. It includes cleansing—the forgiveness that only God can give. And it culminates in availability—the willingness to go wherever God sends, do whatever God asks, become whatever God desires.

Surrender isn't just about giving things up. It's about being sent out. It's about offering ourselves—cleaned up, forgiven, restored—for whatever mission God has in mind.

The Garden Pattern: Jesus Shows Us How

If surrender were easy, Jesus wouldn't have sweat blood.

The night before His crucifixion, Jesus went to the Garden of Gethsemane to pray. Luke tells us that He was in such agony that "his sweat was like drops of blood falling to the ground" (Luke 22:44, NIV). Medical experts say this can actually happen under extreme stress—a condition called hematidrosis, where blood vessels near the sweat glands rupture under intense pressure.

This wasn't calm, collected resignation. This was agonizing struggle.

What was Jesus wrestling with? The cup He was about to drink. The weight of the world's sin about to be placed on His shoulders. The separation from His Father that He would experience on the cross. The physical torture, the emotional abandonment, the spiritual darkness that awaited Him in just a few hours.

And His prayer? "Father, if you are willing, take this cup from me" (Luke 22:42, NIV).

Let that sink in. The Son of God asked if there was another way. The One who had planned the redemption of humanity from before the foundation of the world asked if the plan could be changed. He wasn't pretending to struggle for our benefit. He was genuinely, authentically wrestling with what lay ahead.

But then came the defining words of His life—and the model for ours:

"Yet not my will, but yours be done" (Luke 22:42, NIV).

There it is. The essence of surrender in a sentence. Not my will, but yours.

Notice what Jesus didn't do. He didn't pretend the cup wasn't bitter. He didn't act like surrender was easy or painless. He didn't suppress His emotions or put on a brave face. He was honest with His Father about what He was feeling, about what He wished could be different.

But at the end of the struggle, He chose. He chose His Father's will over His own preference. He chose obedience over comfort. He chose the cross over escape.

This is what surrender looks like in real life. It's not the absence of struggle—it's choosing God's way in the midst of struggle. It's not pretending we don't have preferences—it's releasing our preferences when they conflict with God's purposes. It's being honest about how hard it is and choosing surrender anyway.

If even Jesus wrestled in the garden, we shouldn't be surprised when surrender costs us something. If the Son of God had to consciously choose "not my will, but yours," we can't expect it to come naturally to us either.

The garden pattern is struggle followed by surrender. Honest wrestling followed by willing submission. Expressing our desires followed by releasing them into God's hands.

That's not weakness. That's the kind of strength most of us can barely imagine.

The Great Irony: Purpose Flows from Surrender

Here's something I've observed over thirty-five years of ministry: the people most obsessed with finding white knuckling their way to deciding their purpose are often the least likely to discover it.

They read books about purpose. They take personality assessments. They journal about their passions. They attend seminars and workshops and retreats. They're constantly asking, "What am I supposed to do with my life? What's my calling? Where do I fit?"

And somehow, the answer keeps eluding them.

Meanwhile, I've watched other people—not obsessed with the mental exercise of "picking a purpose"—find exactly what they were made for. Not because they were spending all of their time looking for it, but because they were following Jesus, and Jesus led them to it.

Here's the irony: purpose isn't something we find just because we read something that said we should seek purpose. Purpose is something we discover by seeking God. When we surrender to Him, purpose emerges as a byproduct.

Think about Joseph in the Old Testament. His story is one of the most dramatic in Scripture—sold into slavery by his own brothers, falsely accused and imprisoned in Egypt, forgotten for years in a dungeon. If anyone had reason to obsess about his purpose, it was Joseph. "Why am I here? What's the point of all this suffering? Where is this going?"

But Joseph didn't seem to operate that way. He just kept surrendering. In Potiphar's house, he surrendered his circumstances and did his work with excellence. In prison, he surrendered his bitterness and served the other inmates. In Pharaoh's court, he surrendered his fear and spoke truth to power.

He didn't have a five-year plan. He didn't know how the story would end. He just kept showing up, surrendering each day to whatever God put in front of him.

And in the end? Joseph became the second most powerful man in Egypt, saved his entire family from famine, and preserved the line through which the Messiah would eventually come. His purpose was enormous—literally world-changing. But he didn't discover it by seeking it. He discovered it by surrendering.

Years later, Joseph looked back on the whole journey and summarized it with one of the most profound statements in Scripture: "You intended to harm me, but God intended it for good to accomplish what is now being done, the saving of many lives" (Genesis 50:20, NIV).

That's what happens when we surrender. The broken pieces we didn't understand, the painful chapters that seemed pointless, the delays and detours that frustrated us—they all start making sense. We see how God was weaving our story into His larger narrative all along.

Purpose isn't something we manufacture through goal-setting and strategic planning. It's something God reveals as we yield to Him. Our job isn't to figure out our purpose. Our job is to surrender. Purpose takes care of itself.

Surrender Under Fire: Corrie ten Boom's Story

I want to tell you about a woman whose surrender was tested in the most extreme circumstances imaginable—and whose response still challenges me decades after I first heard her story.

Corrie ten Boom was a Dutch watchmaker, the daughter of a watchmaker, living a quiet life in Haarlem, Netherlands. She was in her late forties when World War II began—well past the age when most people expect adventure. Her life was small and simple: helping her father in his shop, teaching Sunday school, caring for her elderly parent.

Then the Nazis came to Holland.

When the persecution of Jews began, Corrie and her family made a decision that would change everything. They would hide Jews in their home. They would risk their lives to protect people they barely knew. They would surrender their safety, their comfort, their futures to do what was right.

Over the next several years, the ten Boom home became a refuge for countless Jewish people fleeing the Holocaust. They built a secret room—a hiding place behind a false wall in Corrie's bedroom. They developed warning systems and escape routes. They became part of the underground resistance.

In February 1944, an informant betrayed them. The Gestapo raided their home, arrested the entire family, and shipped them off to concentration camps. Corrie's father died within ten days. Her sister Betsie died later at Ravensbrück, a notorious women's camp in Germany.

Corrie herself was released just days before all women her age in the camp were executed. A clerical error, they said later. A miracle, Corrie said.

But here's what makes Corrie's story remarkable: it's not just that she survived. It's what she did with her survival.

After the war, Corrie traveled the world sharing a message of forgiveness and hope. Not bitterness. Not revenge. Forgiveness. She told audiences everywhere that God's love could overcome any hatred, heal any wound, restore any soul.

One night in Munich, after giving a talk on forgiveness, a man approached her. Corrie recognized him immediately—he had been one of the cruelest guards at Ravensbrück. The memories flooded back: her sister's suffering, her own humiliation, the horror of those months in the camp.

The former guard didn't recognize Corrie. He just wanted to shake her hand and thank her for the message about forgiveness. He extended his hand toward her.

Later, Corrie described what happened in that moment. She stood there, frozen, with his hand outstretched. She felt nothing but coldness and bitterness in her heart. She had been preaching forgiveness, but could she practice it? Could she forgive this man who had participated in such evil, who had contributed to her sister's death?

She prayed a desperate prayer: "Jesus, I cannot forgive this man. Give me Your forgiveness."

And then she reached out her hand.

She wrote later that as she took his hand, she felt something like a current passing through her arm, flooding her heart with love for this stranger. The coldness melted. The bitterness released. Forgiveness that was impossible a moment before became real.

That's surrender. Not a feeling but a choice. Not an emotion but an act of the will. Corrie didn't feel like forgiving. She felt like hatred and revenge. But she surrendered her feelings to God and chose to obey anyway.

She described it perfectly: "Forgiveness is an act of the will, and the will can function regardless of the temperature of the heart."

Corrie ten Boom's life demonstrates that surrender isn't a formula for comfort. It's not a strategy for avoiding pain. She suffered terribly—lost her family, her freedom, her health. But surrender gave her something no suffering could steal: a purpose that outlasted her pain and a testimony that has touched millions.

Her most famous quote captures the essence of the surrendered life: "Never be afraid to trust an unknown future to a known God."

That's what surrender looks like when it's put to the test. Not blind optimism. Not denial of difficulty. But trust in a God whose character is settled, even when our circumstances are not. Trust that releases the outcome to Him because we've learned that His hands are safer than ours.

The Invitation Stands

So here we are. We've talked about what surrender is and isn't. We've watched Mary say yes to an angel, Isaiah respond "Here am I," Jesus wrestle in a garden, Joseph trust through decades of delay, and Corrie forgive the unforgivable.

Now comes the uncomfortable part: What about you?

What are you holding onto that God is asking you to release? What plan are you clutching so tightly that there's no room for His plan? What fear is keeping you from saying, "Here am I, send me"?

Maybe it's a dream you've cherished for years—a career path, a relationship outcome, a financial goal. You've built your identity around this dream, and the thought of releasing it feels like releasing yourself.

Maybe it's a wound you can't let go of. Someone hurt you deeply, and forgiveness feels impossible. Your grip on that grievance feels like justice, like protection, like the only power you have left.

Maybe it's a fear—fear of failure, fear of insignificance, fear of what people will think. That fear has been driving your decisions for so long that you can't imagine what life would look like without it.

Maybe it's something more subtle—a preference for comfort, an addiction to control, a need to have all the answers before you take a step.

These aren't dramatic sins, but they're still barriers to the surrendered life.

Whatever it is, God is gently, persistently asking you to open your hands.

Here's what I can promise you: what you're holding onto isn't worth what you're missing out on. The life you've planned isn't as good as the life God has imagined for you. The control you think keeps you safe is actually keeping you stuck.

Paul wrote to the Ephesians about a God who is able to do "immeasurably more than all we ask or imagine, according to his power that is at work within us" (Ephesians 3:20, NIV). Immeasurably more. That's what's on the other side of surrender.

Not always easier. Not always more comfortable. But fuller. Richer. More purposeful. More alive.

The surrendered life is not the diminished life. It's the abundant life Jesus promised. It's the life Mary found in the shadow of an angel's announcement. It's the life Isaiah discovered when he stopped making excuses and started making himself available. It's the life Jesus modeled in a garden, choosing His Father's will over His own survival.

It can be your life too.

What would happen if you opened your hands today? Not someday. Not when you have it all figured out. Not when the circumstances are better or the path is clearer. Today.

"I am the Lord's servant. May your word to me be fulfilled."

"Here am I. Send me."

"Not my will, but yours be done."

The prayer is simple. The decision is yours.

"I am the Lord's servant. May your word to me be fulfilled."
— *Mary of Nazareth*

14

Study Guide: Chapter Three

Personal Reflection Questions

Take time alone with these questions. Be honest. This is between you and God.

Mary said, "I am the Lord's servant." How would you describe your current relationship with God—servant, friend, child, acquaintance, something else? What does your answer reveal about your posture toward Him?

In Isaiah 6, the prophet saw God's holiness and immediately recognized his own sinfulness. When was the last time you had a fresh vision of who God is? How did it affect how you saw yourself?

Jesus prayed in Gethsemane with such intensity that His sweat was like drops of blood. Have you ever wrestled that deeply with God's will? What was the situation, and what was the outcome?

Corrie ten Boom said forgiveness is "an act of the will." Is there someone in your life you need to forgive as an act of surrender, even if your heart isn't there yet? What's holding you back?

This chapter suggests that purpose flows from surrender rather than the other way around. How have you experienced this in your own life? Or, what might God be calling you to surrender so that purpose can emerge?

Group Discussion Questions

For small groups, Sunday school classes, or discussion with a trusted friend.

Read Luke 1:26-38 together. What can we learn from Mary's response to an unexpected and costly calling? What aspects of her example do you find most challenging?

Discuss the difference between surrender as "passivity" and surrender as "active cooperation." Why is this distinction important? How does it change the way you think about following God?

Joseph spent years in prison before his purpose was revealed. How do you stay surrendered when God's plan seems delayed or hidden? What practices or perspectives help you trust during long seasons of waiting?

Corrie ten Boom's story shows that surrender can lead to incredibly difficult places—concentration camps, loss of family, face-to-face encounters with evil. How do we hold together the promise of abundant life with the reality of suffering?

What does it look like practically to live with a "Here am I, send me" posture in daily life? How can we cultivate this kind of availability without neglecting our responsibilities or becoming impractical?

Action Step

This week, write your own "surrender prayer." Structure it around the three movements we saw in Isaiah 6:

Begin with praise—like Isaiah seeing God's holiness, start by focusing on who God is. Write several sentences describing His character, His faithfulness, His majesty.

Move to confession—like Isaiah acknowledging his unclean lips, be honest about your own inadequacy. Confess what's been holding you back from full surrender. Name the fears, the idols, the areas of resistance.

End with availability—like Isaiah saying, "Here am I, send me," offer yourself to God. Tell Him you're willing to go where He sends, do what He asks, become what He desires. Release the outcomes to Him.

Pray this prayer every morning for the next seven days. Keep it where you can see it—on your bathroom mirror, on your dashboard, as the background on your phone. Notice what shifts in your heart as you begin each day with intentional surrender.

The goal isn't to feel something every time you pray it. The goal is to train your will toward surrender, creating a daily habit of opening your hands before God. Over time, this posture becomes part of who you are—not just something you do, but someone you're becoming.

15

CHAPTER FOUR

LIFE IN COMMUNITY

The Acts 2 Blueprint for Transformed Living

Nobody told them they were starting a movement.

The three thousand people who responded to Peter's sermon on Pentecost didn't have a strategic plan. They didn't form a committee. They didn't hire a consultant to help them structure their new organization. They just started living differently—together.

What emerged in those early days in Jerusalem was unlike anything the ancient world had ever witnessed. Luke describes it in Acts 2 with the kind of detail that suggests he knew his readers would have trouble believing it:

"They devoted themselves to the apostles' teaching and to fellowship, to the breaking of bread and to prayer. Everyone was filled with awe at the many wonders and signs performed by the apostles. All the believers were together and had everything in common. They sold property and possessions to give to anyone who had need. Every day they continued to meet together in the temple courts. They broke bread in their homes and ate together with glad and sincere hearts, praising God and enjoying the favor of all the people. And the Lord added to their number daily those who were being saved."

—Acts 2:42-47 (NIV)

Read that passage slowly. Let it sink in. These weren't professional clergy implementing a program. These were ordinary people—fishermen, tax collectors, housewives, merchants—who had encountered the risen Jesus and couldn't go back to life as usual. So, they did the most natural thing in the world: they did life together.

They showed up daily. They shared meals. They opened their wallets and their homes. They learned together, prayed together, laughed together, and probably cried together. And the result? The Lord added to their number daily. Not weekly. Not quarterly. Daily.

Something about the way they lived was so compelling, so attractive, so radically different from the surrounding culture that people couldn't help but take notice. This wasn't a marketing campaign or a growth strategy. It was a lifestyle—and it was irresistible.

Here's what I want you to see as we dive into this chapter: discipleship was never meant to be a solo journey. The surrendered life we've been talking about doesn't happen in isolation. It happens in community—messy, inconvenient, beautiful community.

In the last three chapters, we've looked at recognizing cultural Christianity, counting the cost, and embracing the surrendered life. All of that is essential. But it can still leave you as a lone ranger Christian—trying to follow Jesus by yourself, measuring your progress against your own standards, celebrating your victories alone and nursing your wounds in private.

That's not what Jesus had in mind.

When Jesus called disciples, He called them into a group. When He sent them out, He sent them in pairs. When He prayed His final prayer before the cross, He prayed for their unity. And when the Holy Spirit fell at Pentecost, He didn't fall on individuals scattered across Jerusalem—He fell on a community gathered together in one place.

Community isn't an optional add-on to discipleship. It's the context in which discipleship happens.

The Four Devotions That Changed the World

Luke uses a fascinating word to describe the early church's practice: "devoted." They devoted themselves to four things. Not dabbled in. Not occasionally participated in when it was convenient. Devoted.

The Greek word is proskartereo—a word that carries the idea of persistent, steadfast, single-minded dedication. It's the same word used for a servant who attends constantly to their master, always nearby, always ready, never drifting away. That's the kind of commitment the early church had to these four practices.

And here's what's remarkable: none of these four devotions could be practiced alone.

Devoted to Teaching

The early believers were hungry to learn. They sat under the apostles' instruction, soaking up everything about Jesus—His teachings, His life, His death, His resurrection, and what it all meant for how they should live. This wasn't passive listening; it was active engagement with transforming truth.

Remember, these believers didn't have the New Testament. It hadn't been written yet. What they had was the testimony of men and women who had walked with Jesus, eaten with Him, watched Him die, and encountered Him risen. The apostles' teaching was living history—eyewitness accounts from people whose lives had been turned inside out by the Son of God.

I've been preaching for a LONG time, and I can tell you this: there's a difference between listeners who are present and listeners who are hungry. The early church was hungry. They showed up not because it was expected or because they'd always done it or because someone would notice if they didn't. They showed up because they needed what was being taught like they needed air and water.

Here's the thing about teaching: it's not just about information transfer. It's about formation. Paul told the Romans that we're transformed by the renewing of our minds. When we engage with Scripture in community—hearing it taught, discussing it with others, wrestling with its implications together—something happens that doesn't happen when we're just reading alone. We see things we'd miss. We're challenged in ways we'd avoid. We're held accountable to actually live what we're learning.

Discipleship requires ongoing transformation of the mind. And that transformation happens best in community.

Devoted to Fellowship

Let me be blunt: what most churches call "fellowship" isn't what Luke is describing here.

Coffee and donuts on an occasional Sunday aren't fellowship. A friendly handshake during the "greeting time" isn't fellowship. Small talk about the weather and the football game isn't fellowship. Those things are fine—they're nice—but they're not what the early church was devoted to.

The Greek word here is koinonia, and it means something far deeper. It's the idea of shared life—a deep interconnectedness where what happens to you happens to me. Your burden becomes my burden. Your joy becomes my joy. Your struggle becomes something we face together.

Koinonia is what happens when you call someone at 2 a.m. because your marriage is falling apart—and they answer. It's what happens when you lose your job and your small group shows up with groceries and job leads and prayers. It's what happens when, in your Discipleship Band (details of Discipleship Bands is found at the end of the book), you share about a struggle and instead of judgment, you find arms wrapped around you – and support – and encouragement.

This kind of fellowship is risky. It requires vulnerability. It means letting people see the parts of your life you'd rather keep hidden. But here's what I've learned: the parts of your life you keep in the dark are the parts that keep you stuck. Healing happens in the light of authentic community.

James understood this when he wrote, "Confess your sins to each other and pray for each other so that you may be healed." Notice he didn't say confess your sins to God alone. Of course we do that. But something additional happens when we bring our struggles into the light of trusted community. Isolation is where shame thrives. Fellowship is where healing begins.

Devoted to Breaking Bread

If you want to understand the early church, follow the food.

They broke bread "in their homes" and "ate together with glad and sincere hearts." This was everyday life, not just Sunday morning. They combined the Lord's Supper with ordinary meals, turning dinner tables into sacred space.

Think about that for a moment. In our culture, we've separated the sacred from the secular so completely that we'd never think of communion as something that happens over a pot roast. But the early church didn't make that distinction. Every meal was an opportunity to remember Jesus. Every gathering around a table was a chance to practice the kind of hospitality and generosity that marked their new life in Christ.

There's something powerful about sharing a meal. It's intimate in a way that sitting in rows facing forward isn't. You look each other in the eye. You pass dishes to one another. You linger over conversation. Defenses come down. Walls crumble. Something about food and fellowship together creates space for connection that's hard to find anywhere else.

I've seen more breakthroughs happen around kitchen tables than in any counseling office. There's a reason Jesus ate with sinners, celebrated with friends, and chose a meal as the way He wanted to be remembered.

When was the last time you had someone in your home for a meal who wasn't already family? When was the last time you lingered at the table, not because you had to but because you wanted to? The early church did this daily. It was so central to their identity that "breaking bread" became shorthand for Christian community.

Devoted to Prayer

The church was born in a prayer meeting.

Before Pentecost, Acts 1 tells us that the disciples "all joined together constantly in prayer." They were waiting for the Holy Spirit, and they waited the way Jesus had taught them—on their knees, together. When the Spirit fell, He fell on a praying community. And that community never stopped praying.

Throughout the book of Acts, every major moment is marked by prayer. When they needed to choose a replacement for Judas—they prayed. When Peter and John were arrested and released—they prayed. When famine threatened Jerusalem—they prayed and gave. When Paul and Barnabas were sent out as missionaries—the church prayed and fasted together.

I'm convinced that one of the reasons the American church often lacks power is because we've privatized prayer. We've made it a personal discipline rather than a corporate practice. We pray before meals (sometimes) and before bed (if we remember), but we've largely abandoned the kind of sustained, fervent, corporate prayer that characterized the early church.

Jesus said, "Where two or three gather in my name, there am I with them." There's something about praying together that invites God's presence in a unique way. When we pray in community, we're reminded that we're not alone. We hear others articulate prayers we couldn't find words for. We carry each other's burdens to the throne of grace. We encounter God together.

Private prayer matters. Don't hear me saying it doesn't. But private prayer was never meant to replace corporate prayer—it was meant to complement it. The early church had both, and they were devoted to both.

This Isn't a New Idea: Israel as Community

If you think the Acts 2 community was a brand new invention—some novel experiment in communal living—you haven't spent enough time in the Old Testament.

The Acts 2 church was actually the fulfillment of what God had always intended for His people.

Think about it: when God called Abraham, He wasn't just calling an individual. He was creating a people. "I will make you into a great nation," God promised. From the very beginning, the plan was community.

When God delivered Israel from Egypt, He didn't set up two million individual relationships. He formed a covenant community—a nation bound together by shared identity, shared law, shared worship, and shared responsibility for one another. The laws in Leviticus and Deuteronomy weren't just about personal holiness; they were about creating a distinctive people who cared for each other.

Leave the edges of your field unharvested so the poor can glean. Don't charge interest to fellow Israelites. Forgive debts every seven years. Care for widows and orphans. Welcome the stranger. The whole system was designed to create a community so radically different from surrounding nations that the world would take notice.

God told Israel through Moses, "You will be for me a kingdom of priests and a holy nation." Not a collection of holy individuals—a holy nation. The identity was corporate. The calling was communal.

Israel didn't always live up to this calling, of course. The prophets spent centuries calling them back to covenant faithfulness—not just toward God but toward one another. When Amos thundered against injustice, it was because the community had broken down. When Micah called for mercy and justice, it was because the people had stopped caring for each other. When Malachi confronted their empty worship, it was because they'd kept the rituals while abandoning the relationships.

The Acts 2 church was what Israel was always supposed to be. A community so devoted to God and to one another that the world couldn't ignore them. A people so different from the surrounding culture that others were drawn in by the sheer beauty of their life together.

We're not creating something new when we pursue authentic Christian community. We're stepping into something ancient—as old as Abraham, as deep as the covenant, as wide as God's plan for the ages.

Why You Can't Do This Alone

American Christianity has a problem, and it's a problem most of us don't even see anymore because we're swimming in it.

We've turned "Jesus is my personal Savior" into "Jesus is my private Savior." We've taken the intimate and made it isolated. We've celebrated personal faith to the point where community feels optional—nice if you can get it, but not essential.

The statistics tell the story. Church attendance has declined, but more significantly, in so many places, church involvement has collapsed. Even among those who show up on Sunday, the number who participate in small groups, serve in ministry, or do life together during the week has dropped dramatically. We've become a nation of spectator Christians—watching from a safe distance, connected enough to feel religious but not connected enough to be transformed.

Here's why this matters: the New Testament knows nothing of isolated faith.

Flip through the letters of Paul, Peter, James, and John. You'll find command after command that requires other believers to fulfill. Love one another. Bear one another's burdens. Encourage one another. Forgive one another. Serve one another. Confess your sins to one another. Pray for one another. Teach and admonish one another. Spur one another on toward love and good deeds.

Count them up sometime—there are over fifty "one another" commands in the New Testament. And here's the thing: you can't obey a single one of them by yourself.

Paul used a powerful metaphor to drive this home. He called the church "the body of Christ." Not a collection of individuals who happen to believe the same things. A body—an interconnected organism where every part needs every other part.

"The eye cannot say to the hand, 'I don't need you!'" Paul wrote to the Corinthians. "And the head cannot say to the feet, 'I don't need you!'" Every part matters. Every connection counts. The body only functions when the parts work together.

You can't be the body of Christ by yourself. You just can't. A hand disconnected from the body isn't a body—it's a corpse fragment. An eye floating alone isn't a body—it's a horror movie prop. The very nature of what we're called to be requires connection.

I think about this often: the most important thing you bring to Christian

community is who you've become in your private time with God. But the most important thing you take from community back to your private life is what you've learned by being together. The two aren't in competition—they're in partnership. Solitude without community becomes isolation. Community without solitude becomes superficiality. We need both.

If you're trying to follow Jesus without deep, committed, consistent community, you're attempting something the New Testament never imagined. You might have personal spirituality. You might have religious practices. But you don't have discipleship—not the way Jesus designed it.

The Marks of Authentic Community

So, what does real Christian community look like? How do we move beyond the shallow version we've settled for? I see four essential marks in the Acts 2 church that we desperately need to recover.

Vulnerability

Real community requires taking off our masks.

Most of us spend enormous energy managing our image. We present the version of ourselves we want people to see—the version that has it together, that doesn't struggle much, that's further along the spiritual journey than we actually are. We smile and say "fine" when people ask how we're doing, even when everything is falling apart inside.

The early church couldn't afford that kind of pretense. When you're sharing everything in common, people see behind the curtain pretty quickly. When you're meeting in homes and eating together daily, the facade eventually cracks. They knew each other's messes—and they loved each other anyway.

James 5:16 makes it explicit: "Confess your sins to each other and pray for each other so that you may be healed." Notice the connection—confession leads to healing. The things we keep hidden stay infected. The struggles we bring into the light find relief.

I'm not suggesting we broadcast our deepest struggles to everyone we meet. Vulnerability requires trust, and trust is built over time. But somewhere in your life, you need a handful of people who know the real you—the you behind the Sunday smile—and who love you anyway.

Generosity

The early church "had everything in common. They sold property and possessions to give to anyone who had need."

That sentence should make us uncomfortable. It made the early believers' neighbors uncomfortable too. This was weird. This was radical. This was completely counter-cultural.

I don't think this passage is prescribing a specific economic system. The early church didn't abolish private property—later in Acts, we see believers owning homes and businesses. But they held their possessions loosely. They saw their resources not as "mine" but as "ours." When someone had a need, those with resources stepped up.

This is what generosity looks like in community: not just giving to institutions (though that matters) but giving to people. Noticing when a brother loses his job and showing up with groceries. Seeing a single mom struggling and helping with her car repair. Writing a check when someone's medical bills are crushing them.

Generosity is the natural overflow of hearts that have been transformed by grace. When you realize that everything you have is a gift from God, holding it tightly starts to feel absurd. When you see your brothers and sisters in Christ as actual family, their needs become your concern.

Commitment

They met daily.

I need you to let that sink in. Not weekly. Not when they felt like it. Not when their schedules permitted. Daily.

Now, I understand that first-century Jerusalem isn't twenty-first-century America. People lived differently. Work was organized differently. Distances were shorter. I'm not suggesting you need to gather with your small group or Discipleship Band seven days a week to be a faithful Christian.

But here's what I am suggesting: authentic community requires showing up consistently, even when you don't feel like it.

In our consumer culture, we've been trained to participate only when it's convenient and satisfying. If the small group discussion isn't stimulating, we find something better to do. If the Sunday gathering isn't meeting our needs absolutely every week, we sleep in. We approach community like we approach streaming services—consuming when we want, disengaging when we don't.

But relationships don't work that way. Marriage doesn't work that way. Friendship doesn't work that way. And Christian community doesn't work that way either.

The deepest relationships in your life are built through consistent presence over time. They're forged in the ordinary moments, not just the mountain-top experiences. The trust that enables vulnerability comes from showing up again and again, proving through presence that you're not going anywhere.

Commitment means putting community on your calendar and protecting it. It means being there for others even when no one's there for you in that particular moment. It means deciding in advance that this matters, so you're not making the decision fresh every week based on how you feel.

Mission

Here's the part we often miss: the Acts 2 community wasn't inward-focused. They weren't circling the wagons, protecting themselves from the big bad world. They were so attractive that "the Lord added to their number daily those who were being saved."

The community itself was their witness.

Think about what this looked like from the outside. In a world defined by ethnic divisions and social hierarchies, here was a group where Jews and Gentiles ate together. Masters and slaves worshiped side by side. Rich and poor shared resources without keeping score. Men and women served alongside one another. The usual walls didn't exist.

People noticed. How could they not? This was revolutionary. This was bizarre. This was beautiful.

Jesus had predicted this. In His prayer the night before the cross, He prayed for His followers' unity—"that all of them may be one, Father, just as you are in me and I am in you." And then He gave the reason: "so that the world may believe that you have sent me."

Our unity—our love for one another—is our most powerful evangelistic tool. When the world sees Christians who genuinely care for each other, who sacrifice for each other, who stick together through hard times, it creates a curiosity that opens doors for the gospel.

Authentic community is never just about us. It's always oriented outward—toward the needs of a world that desperately wants to belong somewhere. The best communities I've seen are the ones that leave an empty seat at the table. They're always looking for the next person to include, the next neighbor to welcome, the next seeker to embrace.

Small But Not Alone: Mother Teresa's Vision

In 1948, a small woman left the relative comfort of her teaching position at a convent school in Calcutta to serve "the poorest of the poor" in the city's slums. She had no funding. No organization. No strategic plan. She had only a calling—and she knew she couldn't do it alone.

Mother Teresa understood something essential about world-changing mission: it requires community.

Within two years, she had gathered a group of young women around the vision, and the Missionaries of Charity was born. Over the following decades, this tiny community would grow into a global movement of thousands of sisters, brothers, and priests—all bound together by devotion to Jesus and the poor.

What strikes me about the Missionaries of Charity is how Acts 2 their rhythm is. They pray together—daily, for hours. They eat together. They serve together. They own nothing individually; everything belongs to the community. Their life together is marked by the same devotion Luke described in the early church.

Mother Teresa didn't try to be a lone hero saving the world single-handedly. She built a community. She gathered people around a shared mission. And together, they accomplished what none of them could have accomplished alone.

"I can do things you cannot," she once observed, "you can do things I cannot; together we can do great things."

That's not just a nice sentiment—it's biblical theology. We are the body of Christ, and the body only functions when the parts work together. The eye needs the hand. The hand needs the foot. No part is complete on its own.

When Mother Teresa received the Nobel Peace Prize in 1979, she didn't use her acceptance speech to talk about herself. She talked about Jesus. She talked about the poor. She talked about the community of sisters who served alongside her. She understood that whatever impact her life had was never about her as an individual—it was about what God could do through surrendered people bound together in love.

Most of us will never start a global movement. But all of us need community to become who we're called to be. All of us need brothers and sisters who will walk with us, challenge us, encourage us, and hold us accountable. All of us need what the early church had—and what Mother Teresa built.

Where Will You Find Your People?

I want to close this chapter with a practical question: Where are you finding your Acts 2 community?

Maybe you're already there. Maybe you've got a small group, a Sunday school class, a circle of friends who do life together in authentic, committed community. If so, thank God for them. Don't take them for granted. Invest in those relationships like your spiritual life depends on it—because it does.

But maybe you're reading this and realizing you don't have that. You attend church—maybe faithfully—but you're still essentially alone. You know people, but nobody really knows you. You haven't found your people.

If that's you, I want you to hear two things.

First: this isn't going to happen by accident. Authentic community rarely falls into your lap. You have to pursue it. You have to be willing to take initiative, to be awkward, to risk rejection. You have to show up consistently even before it feels rewarding. You have to invest before you see returns.

Second: sometimes you have to become the community you're looking for. Maybe God is calling you not just to find a group but to start one. Maybe He's positioning you to gather people who are just as hungry for authentic connection as you are.

The Acts 2 church didn't wait for someone else to organize them. They just started doing life together. They opened their homes. They shared their meals. They prayed together and studied together and served together. And what emerged was something so beautiful that the world couldn't ignore it.

You were not meant to follow Jesus alone. The Christian life was never designed as a solo performance—it's a symphony. God is calling you not just to personal transformation but to participate in a community that displays His kingdom to the world.

So, here's my challenge: before you turn the page, answer this question—who will you do life with? Who are the people God is calling you to pursue deeper relationship with? Who needs you to show up for them?

Write their names down. Pray over them. Then reach out. Invite someone to coffee. Host a dinner. Join a group. Start one if you have to.

The world is waiting for communities of believers who love each other so well that people take notice. The world is hungry for what the early church had—even if they don't know to call it that.

Be that community. Find your people. Do life together.

This is how disciples are made.

———————————

"They devoted themselves to the apostles' teaching and to fellow-ship, to the breaking of bread and to prayer."
— *Acts 2:42 (NIV)*

16

Study Guide: Chapter Four

Personal Reflection Questions

Take time alone with these questions. Be honest. This is between you and God.

Of the four devotions of the Acts 2 church—teaching, fellowship, breaking bread, and prayer—which is strongest in your life right now? Which is weakest? What would it look like to grow in your weakest area?

The early church met daily and shared everything. How does your current church involvement compare? What barriers—time, fear, past hurt, busyness—keep you from deeper community?

When was the last time you were truly vulnerable with another believer—sharing about a struggle, admitting a failure, asking for help? What holds you back from that kind of authenticity? What would you need to feel safe enough to open up?

This chapter suggests that solitary time with God and community time with others work together. How do these two aspects of spiritual life reinforce each other in your experience? Are you neglecting one at the expense of the other?

Who are the people God has placed in your life who could become deeper "Acts 2" community? Write down their names. What would it take to move those relationships toward greater authenticity and commitment?

Group Discussion Questions

For small groups, Sunday school classes, or discussion with a trusted friend.

Read Acts 2:42-47 together. What strikes you most about this description of the early church? What seems most attractive about this community? What seems most challenging to replicate in our modern context?

Discuss the statement: "American Christianity has been infected by individualism." Do you agree? What evidence do you see? How has individualism shaped your own approach to faith? What can we do to combat this tendency?

The early church "had everything in common." What would radical generosity look like in your context? What keeps us from sharing more freely with one another—fear, pride, the belief that what we have is "ours"?

Why do you think the Acts 2 community was so attractive to outsiders that "the Lord added to their number daily"? What would make our church communities more compelling to people who don't yet know Jesus?

Mother Teresa said, "I can do things you cannot, you can do things I cannot; together we can do great things." Share an experience where Christian community enabled you to do something you couldn't have done alone. How has belonging to the body of Christ made you more than you would have been as an individual?

Action Step

This week, take one concrete step toward deeper community. Choose one of these options—or create your own—and do it before the week ends:

Option 1: Invite someone from church to share a meal in your home. Not a fancy dinner party—just a simple meal around your table. Focus on listening and getting to know them at a deeper level.

Option 2: If you aren't in a Discipleship Band – ask 3-4 people (all men or all women) to join you in forming a group. Set you times to meet (weekly or every other week) and begin the process of getting to know each other better, and supporting each other in your walk with Christ.

Option 3: If you're not currently part of a small group or Sunday school class, commit to joining one. Don't wait until you feel ready or until you find the perfect group. Just start showing up.

Option 4: Identify one person you will intentionally connect with every week—a phone call, a text, a coffee. Build consistent presence over time. Show up for someone, and let them show up for you.

The goal isn't to check a box—it's to take a step. Authentic community is built through many small, faithful steps taken over time. This week, take one of them.

Remember: you were not designed for isolation. You were created for community. And the life of a surrendered disciple is a life lived with others.

17

CHAPTER FIVE

ON MISSION WITH GOD

Living as Salt and Light in a World that Needs Hope

It wasn't a suggestion.

When Jesus stood on that mountain in Galilee, looking into the faces of the eleven remaining disciples, He didn't offer them a polite invitation to consider mission work if their schedules permitted. He didn't say, "Some of you might want to think about sharing this message when you get a chance." He didn't qualify His words with "for those who feel called" or "if it's not too inconvenient."

He issued a command.

"All authority in heaven and on earth has been given to me. Therefore go and make disciples of all nations, baptizing them in the name of the Father and of the Son and of the Holy Spirit, and teaching them to obey everything I have commanded you. And surely I am with you always, to the very end of the age." (Matthew 28:18-20, NIV)

Notice the structure. Jesus begins with a staggering claim of authority—all authority in heaven and on earth. Then comes the word "therefore." Because Jesus has all authority, because He is who He says He is, because the resurrection has proven everything—therefore go.

The going flows from the knowing. The mission flows from the identity of the One who sends us. We don't go because we're adequate; we go because He is authoritative.

And here's what I want you to see: this commission wasn't given to a special subset of super-spiritual disciples. It wasn't reserved for professional clergy or those with theological degrees. It was given to ordinary people who had walked with Jesus for three years—fishermen, tax collectors, everyday folks who had said yes to following Him.

The same commission extends to you.

In the previous chapters, we've talked about waking up from cultural Christianity, counting the cost, embracing the surrendered life, and living in community. All of that is essential. But here's where the rubber meets the road: discipleship that doesn't lead to mission isn't discipleship at all. We are not saved to sit. We are not transformed for our own comfort. We are not gathered in community just to enjoy each other's company.

We are saved, transformed, and gathered to be sent.

A disciple who doesn't participate in God's mission is a contradiction in terms. It's like saying you're a swimmer who never gets in the water or a musician who never plays an instrument. The very definition of what we are includes what we do—and what we do is carry the good news of Jesus to a world that desperately needs hope.

So, here's the question this chapter puts before you: Are you on mission?

The Mission of God

Before there was a church on mission, there was God on mission.

This is one of the most important things I've learned over the years: we don't bring God to our mission. We join God in His. The mission doesn't originate with us—it originates with Him. He's been at it since the beginning, and He graciously invites us to participate.

Think about it. In Genesis 3, after Adam and Eve had sinned and hidden themselves in shame, who went looking for whom? God came walking through the garden, calling out, "Where are you?" He already knew where they were, of course. The question wasn't for His information—it was an invitation. Even in the moment of their greatest failure, God pursued.

And He's been pursuing ever since.

The whole Bible, from Genesis to Revelation, tells the story of a missionary God—a God who refuses to leave His creation in its brokenness, who keeps reaching out, who sacrifices everything to bring His children home. He called Abraham out of Ur. He sent Moses back to Egypt. He raised up prophets to speak to stubborn Israel. He ultimately sent His own Son to do what no one else could do.

Theologians sometimes call this the Missio Dei—the mission of God. It's a helpful phrase because it reminds us where the mission comes from. We didn't invent it. We can't improve on it. We can only join it or stand on the sidelines.

Understanding this changes everything about how we approach mission. When mission is something we do for God, it becomes about our efforts, our results, our strategies. We feel the weight of success or failure on our shoulders. We burn out. We keep score. We compare our ministries to each other.

But when we understand that mission is God's activity that we're invited into, the pressure shifts. We're not responsible for outcomes—He is. We're not the lead actors—we're supporting cast in His drama. Our job is to show up, say yes, and let Him work through us.

This doesn't mean we don't work hard. It means we work from rest instead of for rest. We serve from overflow instead of obligation. We step out in faith knowing that the God who sends us is the same God who goes before us, who walks beside us, and who will complete what He started.

You're not launching a mission for God. You're joining a mission that's been underway since before you were born. The only question is whether you'll say yes.

Blessed to Be a Blessing: Abraham's Missional Call

We talked about Abraham back in Chapter Two when we were counting the cost. Remember—he left everything familiar, stepped out in faith, and followed God to an unknown destination. That took courage. That required surrender.

But there's something about Abraham's call we need to revisit, because it contains a principle that shapes everything we're talking about in this chapter.

When God called Abraham, He made a promise: "I will make you into a great nation, and I will bless you; I will make your name great, and you will be a blessing. I will bless those who bless you, and whoever curses you I will curse; and all peoples on earth will be blessed through you." (Genesis 12:2-3, NIV)

Did you catch that? God promised to bless Abraham—but the blessing had a purpose. It wasn't meant to end with him. The blessing was designed to flow through him to "all peoples on earth."

Abraham was blessed to be a blessing.

This is the pattern of the kingdom. God doesn't bless us so we can stockpile blessings like a squirrel hoarding acorns. He blesses us so we can become conduits of blessing to others. Whatever He gives us—salvation, transformation, spiritual gifts, material resources, influence, opportunities—is meant to flow through us to a world in need.

Think about what God has given you. Your salvation. Your story. Your testimony of how Jesus changed your life. The peace you've found. The forgiveness you've received. The hope that sustains you. None of that was meant to stay bottled up inside you like a spiritual trophy collection.

It was meant to overflow.

Israel, Abraham's descendants, was supposed to understand this. They were chosen not for privilege but for responsibility. They were meant to be "a light for the Gentiles," a display case for God's glory, an advertisement for what it looks like when a people truly belong to the living God. Their holiness, their community, their worship—all of it was supposed to draw the surrounding nations to the God they served.

Too often, they forgot. They turned inward. They hoarded the blessing instead of sharing it. They built walls instead of bridges. And the nations never saw what they were supposed to see.

The church faces the same temptation today. We can become so focused on receiving blessings that we forget we're supposed to be giving them away. We build bigger buildings for ourselves instead of bigger tables for others. We measure success by what we have instead of what we've given.

Here's a question worth sitting with: What has God blessed you with? And who is meant to be blessed through you?

That person's face that just flashed through your mind? That's probably not an accident.

Salt and Light: Jesus's Vision for His Followers

Early in His ministry, Jesus climbed a mountain and sat down to teach. What followed—the Sermon on the Mount—is the most concentrated collection of Jesus's teaching in all of Scripture. It's the manifesto of the kingdom, the constitution of the new community Jesus was forming.

And right at the beginning, He told His followers who they were:

"You are the salt of the earth. But if the salt loses its saltiness, how can it be made salty again? It is no longer good for anything, except to be thrown out and trampled underfoot. You are the light of the world. A town built on a hill cannot be hidden. Neither do people light a lamp and put it under a bowl. Instead they put it on its stand, and it gives light to everyone in the house. In the same way, let your light shine before others, that they may see your good deeds and glorify your Father in heaven." (Matthew 5:13-16, NIV)

Two metaphors. Salt and light. Both of them active. Both of them missional. Both of them pointing outward.

Let's think about salt for a moment. In Jesus's day, salt served three primary purposes: it preserved food from decay, it enhanced flavor, and it created thirst. A piece of meat without salt would rot quickly in the Middle Eastern heat. A meal without salt tasted flat and lifeless. And anyone who's ever eaten salty food knows it makes you want to drink.

Now apply that to the life of a disciple. As salt, we're meant to preserve—to slow the decay of a culture that's rotting from the inside out, to stand for truth and righteousness in a world that's abandoned both. We're meant to enhance—to bring flavor and fullness to life, to show people what it looks like when humans actually live the way we were designed to live. And we're meant to create thirst—to make people want what we have, to make them curious about the source of our peace, our joy, our hope.

But here's the thing about salt: it's useless if it stays in the shaker. Salt has to leave the container to make things better. It has to get out of the saltshaker. Salt that never touches anything is just a decoration.

Then there's light. Light illuminates. It reveals what's hidden in darkness. It guides people who've lost their way. It drives out fear. Light doesn't argue with darkness—it just shines, and darkness has to retreat.

Jesus didn't say we should try to become salt and light. He said we are salt and light. This is our identity, not just our activity. The question isn't whether we're meant to affect our environment—that's settled. The question is whether we actually will make things better and brighter.

Jesus warns about salt losing its saltiness and light being hidden under a bowl. Both images describe the same tragic reality: disciples who refuse to engage with the world around them. We can lose our saltiness by so accommodating ourselves to the culture that we become indistinguishable from it—same values, same priorities, same obsessions, just with a thin Christian veneer. Or we can hide our light by so separating ourselves from the culture that we never actually influence anyone—safe in our Christian bubbles, surrounded by Christian friends, consuming Christian media, invisible to everyone who needs what we have.

Neither option fulfills what we're called to.

Disciples are meant to be in the world—flavoring it, shining into it, influencing it—without being of the world. We're embedded agents of transformation, not isolated protectors of our own self-righteous purity.

Where is God asking you to be salt today? Where is He asking you to let your light shine? Where should you be making things better? Where are the opportunities for you to make things brighter?

The Unstoppable Mission: Power from Pentecost

The book of Acts is the story of ordinary people doing extraordinary things.

If you've ever thought you weren't qualified for mission—weren't educated enough, weren't eloquent enough, weren't spiritual enough—the early church should give you hope. These weren't religious professionals with seminary degrees. They were fishermen and tax collectors, tentmakers and merchants, slaves and free, men and women who had one thing in common: they'd encountered the risen Jesus and been filled with His Spirit.

And they couldn't keep it to themselves.

On the Day of Pentecost, the Holy Spirit fell on the gathered believers, and they spilled out into the streets of Jerusalem speaking in languages they'd never learned. Peter—the same Peter who had denied Jesus three times just weeks earlier—stood up and preached with such power that three thousand people gave their lives to Christ in a single day.

That was just the beginning.

In Acts 8, persecution scattered the believers from Jerusalem, and everywhere they went, they shared the gospel. Philip ended up in Samaria—enemy territory for any good Jew—and a revival broke out. Then the Spirit sent him to a desert road where an Ethiopian official just happened to be reading Isaiah and needed someone to explain it. Philip shared Jesus, baptized the man on the spot, and the gospel headed toward Africa.

In Acts 10, Peter received a vision that shattered his assumptions about who was eligible for salvation. He went to the house of Cornelius, a Roman centurion, and watched the Holy Spirit fall on Gentiles for the first time. The walls were coming down. The good news was spreading beyond every boundary.

Then there was Paul—the former persecutor turned apostle—who carried the gospel to the ends of the known world. He planted churches in major cities across the Roman Empire, wrote letters that would become Scripture, trained up leaders, and eventually gave his life for the message he once tried to destroy.

What made these ordinary people so effective? It wasn't strategy, though they were strategic. It wasn't organization, though they organized. It was the fact that they couldn't help but share what they'd experienced.

When the authorities arrested Peter and John and commanded them to stop speaking about Jesus, their response was classic: "We cannot help speaking about what we have seen and heard" (Acts 4:20, NIV). They weren't being defiant for defiance's sake. They were being honest. When you've really encountered Jesus, silence isn't an option.

After their release, the believers gathered and prayed. And here's what they prayed for—not safety, not protection, not for the persecution to stop. They prayed for boldness. "Now, Lord, consider their threats and enable your servants to speak your word with great boldness" (Acts 4:29, NIV).

That prayer still echoes down through the centuries. The early church didn't pray for comfort—they prayed for courage. They didn't ask God to remove the obstacles—they asked Him to empower them to speak anyway.

The result? "They were all filled with the Holy Spirit and spoke the word of God boldly" (Acts 4:31, NIV). And the gospel spread like wildfire.

I wonder what would happen if we prayed the same prayer today. Not "Lord, make my life easier" but "Lord, make me bolder." Not "Lord, remove my obstacles" but "Lord, give me courage to speak anyway."

Your Mission Field Is Already Around You

Here's a mistake I've seen Christians make for decades: they think mission is only something that happens somewhere else.

Yes, it's true that mission trips often happen in other communities, other states, or other countries. There are times and opportunities for us to cross the county line, the state lie, or to cross an ocean. Those times are amazing and transformational. So, if God is calling you to cross into one of those areas – by all means – do it!

But here's the truth most of us need to hear: everyone is called to cross the street.

Your mission field is also wherever you already are. Your neighborhood is a mission field. Your workplace is a mission field. Your gym, your kids' school, your favorite coffee shop, your social media feeds—all mission fields. You don't need to go anywhere special to be on mission. You just need to open your eyes to where you already are.

Think about the people you interact with on a regular basis. The coworker who's going through a divorce and doesn't know who to talk to. The neighbor whose is struggling to keep up appearances in a community they can't afford. The friend who's successful by every worldly measure but seems vaguely empty inside. The family member who's never understood why faith matters to you and has never asked—but might if you gave them an opening.

These are your people. This is your mission field.

Mission doesn't require a microphone or a platform or a fancy strategy. It often just requires paying attention—noticing the person in front of you, asking the second question instead of just the first, being genuinely curious about people's stories. It requires availability—making time for relationships that don't immediately benefit you, being present when someone needs to talk, showing up when it's inconvenient.

And eventually, mission requires words. We can't just live good lives and hope people figure out why. At some point, we need to tell them about Jesus—who He is, what He's done, what He means to us. Not in a preachy, uncomfortable, forced way. But in the natural overflow of a relationship where they already know you care.

The old preacher Charles Spurgeon once put it bluntly: every Christian is either a missionary or an impostor. That sounds harsh but think about what he meant. If you've really experienced the grace of Jesus—if you've really been rescued from darkness and brought into light—how can you keep that to yourself? If you knew the cure for a disease that was killing everyone around you, wouldn't you share it?

The question isn't whether you're called to mission. The question is whether you'll wake up to the mission field God has already placed you in.

A Life on Mission: William Wilberforce

I want to tell you about a man who almost missed his mission field because he was looking in the wrong place.

William Wilberforce was a young British politician with a bright future. He'd been elected to Parliament at just twenty-one years old, was a gifted speaker, and counted the prime minister among his close friends. By every measure, he was a rising star in eighteenth-century British politics.

Then everything changed. In his mid-twenties, Wilberforce underwent a profound conversion to Christianity. His faith went from nominal to transformative, and suddenly he saw everything differently—including his career.

Wilberforce began to wonder if he should leave politics altogether. Shouldn't a serious Christian devote himself to ministry? Wasn't Parliament too corrupt, too worldly, too compromised for someone who wanted to follow Jesus wholeheartedly? Maybe he should step away from public life and focus on spiritual things.

He sought counsel from John Newton—yes, the same John Newton who wrote "Amazing Grace." Newton had been a slave ship captain before his dramatic conversion, and he knew something about grace meeting a person in unexpected places.

Newton's advice surprised Wilberforce. He told him to stay in politics. He saw Wilberforce's position not as an obstacle to faith but as a platform for it. God had placed him in Parliament for a reason. His mission field wasn't somewhere else—it was right where he was.

Wilberforce listened. He stayed. And he took on what would become his life's work: the abolition of the slave trade.

It took decades. Year after year, Wilberforce introduced bills to abolish the trade in human beings. Year after year, he was defeated. The slave trade was enormously profitable. Powerful interests opposed him. Some said it couldn't be done. Others said it shouldn't be done. He was mocked, criticized, threatened.

But Wilberforce was a man on mission, and men on mission don't give up easily.

He worked tirelessly to change hearts and minds. He gathered evidence. He built coalitions. He appealed to conscience. He connected faith to justice, showing his countrymen that the God they claimed to worship cared about the African men, women, and children being torn from their homes and shipped in chains across the Atlantic.

One of his most famous statements captures his moral clarity: "You may choose to look the other way, but you can never say again that you did not know."

In 1807, after nearly twenty years of effort, Parliament finally passed the Abolition of the Slave Trade Act. The slave trade was illegal throughout the British Empire. Wilberforce was in the chamber when the vote was announced, and his colleagues gave him a standing ovation, tears streaming down many of their faces.

But Wilberforce wasn't done. He spent the rest of his life working toward the abolition of slavery itself—not just the trade but the institution. In 1833, just three days before he died, Parliament passed the Slavery Abolition Act, freeing all slaves throughout the British Empire.

What if Wilberforce had left Parliament? What if he'd decided that politics was too worldly for a serious Christian? Millions of people might have remained in chains. History might have taken a very different course.

His life demonstrates something we desperately need to understand: mission takes different forms. For some, it's crossing oceans. For others, it's staying put and transforming the sphere of influence God has already given them. The question isn't whether your mission looks like someone else's. The question is whether you're faithful to the mission God has given you.

Your Parliament may not look like Wilberforce's. Your cause may not make history books. But you have a sphere of influence—relationships, opportunities, a platform of some kind—and God has placed you there for a reason.

Don't miss your mission field by looking for it somewhere else.

The Invitation Awaits

God's mission is moving forward. It has been since that first walk through the garden, calling out to His hiding children. It was moving through Abraham, through Israel, through prophets and priests and kings. It exploded into the world through Jesus and continues through His Spirit-empowered church.

And now the invitation comes to you.

The question isn't whether you're qualified—you're not, and neither was anyone else God has ever used. Peter was impulsive and unreliable. Moses was a murderer with a speech impediment. David was an adulterer. Paul was a persecutor of the church. None of them had it together. All of them were used.

The question is whether you're willing.

What if you started seeing every interaction as a potential divine appointment? What if you began each morning asking God, "Who do You want me to reach today? Who needs to see Your love through me?" What if you paid attention to the needs around you instead of scrolling past them? What if you spoke up about your faith when opportunities presented themselves?

The world is waiting. Not for perfect Christians—they don't exist. Not for professional ministers—there aren't enough of them to go around. The world is waiting for ordinary disciples who are willing to be salt and light wherever they are. The world is waiting for people who've tasted grace and can't keep it to themselves.

Your neighbor is waiting. Your coworker is waiting. Your family member who's never understood faith is waiting. They may not know they're waiting, but they are. They're waiting for someone to show them that God is real, that hope is possible, that there's more to life than the emptiness they feel.

Could that someone be you?

I'm reminded of something a missionary once said that has stayed with me for years. He observed that only what's done for Christ will last—that we have one life, and it will soon be past. Everything else we accomplish, accumulate, and achieve will eventually fade. Only what we invest in eternity has eternal returns.

You have one life. It will soon be past. What are you doing with it?

The Great Commission is still great. The mission of God is still moving. The world still needs hope. And Jesus is still saying what He said to those first disciples on a mountain in Galilee:

"Go."

Will you?

"Therefore go and make disciples of all nations."

—*Jesus of Nazareth*

18

Study Guide: Chapter Five

Personal Reflection Questions

Take time alone with these questions. Be honest. This is between you and God.

If someone observed your life for a week, would they see evidence that you're "on mission" with God? What specific things would they notice? What would be missing?

Jesus called His followers salt and light. Which metaphor resonates more with your current calling? How are you bringing preservation and seasoning (salt) or illumination and guidance (light) to your environment? How are you making your world better and brighter?

Think about your "mission field"—your home, workplace, neighborhood, and social circles. Who in those spaces doesn't know Jesus? Write down their names. When was the last time you prayed specifically for their salvation?

Wilberforce almost left politics for "ministry" before being convinced to stay and influence from within. Where might God be calling you to stay and transform rather than leave? How might your current position be your mission field?

What fears or obstacles keep you from being more active in God's mission? Name them specifically. What would help you overcome them? What would change if you prayed for boldness like the early church did?

Group Discussion Questions

For small groups, Sunday school classes, or discussion with a trusted friend.

Read Matthew 28:18-20 together. What strikes you about the scope and tone of Jesus's command? How does the phrase "all authority has been given to me" change how we approach the command to "go"? How should this shape our priorities as individuals and as a church?

Discuss the concept of "Missio Dei"—that mission is God's activity that we join rather than something we initiate. How does this perspective change how we think about evangelism and outreach? Does it relieve pressure, or does it increase responsibility?

God told Abraham he would be blessed to be a blessing. In what ways has God blessed you? How might those specific blessings be meant to flow through you to others? Are you hoarding any blessings that were meant to be shared?

The early church prayed for boldness when facing opposition (Acts 4:29). What would bold faith look like in your context today? What keeps us from praying that prayer—and meaning it? What might God do if we started praying for courage instead of comfort?

Spurgeon said every Christian is either "a missionary or an impostor." Is this statement too strong, or is it an accurate reflection of what Jesus expects? How do you respond to this challenge? What adjustments might your group need to make to live more missionally?

Action Step

This week, identify one person in your sphere of influence who doesn't know Jesus. Write their name down. Commit to praying for them daily for the next 30 days—not just general prayers, but specific prayers for their heart to be opened to the gospel.

As you pray, look for opportunities to serve them, build relationship, and demonstrate Christ's love in practical ways. Don't force spiritual conversations—let them emerge naturally from genuine care. But when an opening comes, be ready to share your story of what Jesus has done in your life.

Ask God for the courage to be salt and light in their life. Ask Him to make you sensitive to their needs and alert to divine appointments.

Keep a journal of what you notice over the 30 days—both in them and in yourself.

Remember: you're not responsible for converting anyone. That's the Holy Spirit's work. You're responsible for showing up, loving well, and speaking when He prompts you. Leave the results to God.

Your mission field is already around you. Open your eyes. Step into it. See what God does.

19

CHAPTER SIX

THE BOLD YES

A Call to Faithfulness in a World that Needs Your Yes

The water didn't part first.

I know we usually tell the story as if it did. We imagine the Jordan River splitting dramatically, creating a dry highway through the middle, and then the Israelites marching confidently across to claim their promised land. It makes for a clean, comfortable narrative—miracle first, obedience second.

But that's not how it happened.

The people of Israel had been wandering in the wilderness for forty years. An entire generation had been born and raised knowing nothing but desert sand and manna from heaven. They had heard the stories about Egypt, about the Red Sea crossing, about the God who delivered their parents from Pharaoh's army. But they had never seen the Promised Land with their own eyes.

Now, finally, it was in sight. Canaan lay just across the Jordan River. Everything they had been waiting for, everything their parents and grandparents had dreamed about, was right there. One river stood between them and their destiny.

And the Jordan was at flood stage.

This wasn't a gentle stream they could wade across. The spring rains had swollen the river beyond its banks, turning it into a churning, dangerous torrent. Under normal circumstances, crossing would have been risky. Under these circumstances, it looked impossible.

Then God spoke to Joshua, Moses' successor, with instructions that must have made his stomach drop: "Tell the priests who carry the ark of the covenant: 'When you reach the edge of the Jordan's waters, go and stand in the river.'"

Stand in the river. Not "wait until the river parts" or "watch from a safe distance until I make a path." Go stand in the flood.

Joshua gathered the people and told them what was about to happen: "This is how you will know that the living God is among you... As soon as the priests who carry the ark of the Lord—the Lord of all the earth—set foot in the Jordan, its waters flowing downstream will be cut off and stand up in a heap."

Did you catch that? As soon as the priests set foot in the Jordan. Not before. The miracle was contingent on obedience. The water would part when—and only when—they stepped in.

I've tried to imagine what that moment felt like for those priests. They were carrying the most sacred object in Israel—the Ark of the Covenant, representing the very presence of God. They were leading two million people toward a swollen river with only a promise that things would change once their feet got wet.

What if it doesn't work? What if we misunderstood? What if we step in and nothing happens?

They stepped in anyway.

Joshua chapter three tells us that "as soon as the priests who carried the ark reached the Jordan and their feet touched the water's edge, the water from upstream stopped flowing." The river piled up in a heap far upstream, and the priests stood on dry ground in the middle of the riverbed while the entire nation crossed over.

Here's what I want you to see: God often works this way. He doesn't part the waters so we'll have the courage to step in. He parts the waters when we step in. The miracle follows the faith. The provision comes after the obedience.

This is the pattern of the kingdom. Abraham had to leave Ur before he knew where he was going. Moses had to confront Pharaoh before the plagues began. David had to run toward Goliath before the stone found its mark. Mary had to say yes to the angel before she understood how any of it would work.

And you—you have to step into the water before the path appears.

God is looking for people with wet feet. People who trust Him enough to move before all the questions are answered. People who say yes and then watch Him work.

That's what this chapter is about. We've covered a lot of ground in this book—recognizing cultural Christianity, counting the cost, embracing surrender, finding community, living on mission. But all of that learning means nothing if it doesn't lead somewhere. At some point, the journey of understanding has to become the journey of action.

The Jordan is in front of you. The question is whether you'll step in.

The Journey We've Traveled

Let's take a moment to remember where we've been.

We started in the Introduction with an invitation—the same invitation Jesus has been extending for two thousand years. "Follow Me." Not just "believe in Me" as a theological fact. Not "add Me to your schedule." Follow Me. Leave what you're holding and step into something new.

In Chapter One, we got honest about where many of us actually are. We looked in the mirror and recognized the signs of cultural Christianity—faith by geography, compartmentalized belief, consumer Christianity, moralistic therapeutic deism, checking-the-box religion, risk-free faith, private spirituality. Not to condemn, but to create awareness. You can't get somewhere new until you acknowledge where you're starting from.

Chapter Two took us into the hard sayings of Jesus—the ones we tend to skip because they make us uncomfortable. We counted the cost. We looked at what Jesus actually asks of His followers: reordered priorities that put Him above everything and everyone else, daily cross-bearing that means dying to self over and over, and total surrender that holds nothing back. The cost is real. We needed to see that clearly.

But then in Chapter Three, we discovered the great paradox. Surrender isn't about losing yourself—it's about finding yourself. When we yield to God's plan, we don't become less; we become more. Purpose doesn't come from seeking purpose; it comes from seeking God. The surrendered life is the discovered life.

Chapter Four pulled us out of isolation and into community. We saw the Acts 2 church as our blueprint—devoted to teaching, fellowship, breaking bread, and prayer. We recognized that discipleship was never meant to be a solo journey. We need each other. The body of Christ only functions when the parts work together.

And in Chapter Five, we stepped into mission. We remembered that we're saved to be sent, blessed to be a blessing, called to be salt and light in a world that desperately needs hope. Our mission field isn't only somewhere far away—it's wherever we already are.

That's the journey. The opportunity to wrestle with what it means to move from cultural Christianity to surrendered discipleship. Six chapters of confronting comfortable assumptions and embracing uncomfortable truths.

Now comes the question that matters most: What will you do with all of this?

The Invitation: Say Yes

God isn't looking for perfect people. He's never been looking for perfect people. If He were, He'd still be looking, because perfect people don't exist.

What God is looking for are available people. Willing people. People who raise their hand and say, "Here am I—send me," even when they don't feel qualified, even when they can't see the whole path, even when everything in them wants to stay safe and comfortable.

Think about the people God has used throughout Scripture. Not one of them had it together.

Abraham was an average guy in Ur before God called him. Moses was a murderer with a speech impediment who spent forty years hiding in the desert. Rahab was a prostitute. David was an adulterer who had a man killed to cover his sin. Peter was impulsive and, at times, unreliable—the guy who denied Jesus three times. Paul spent years persecuting the church before he became its greatest missionary.

These weren't polished, put-together people. They were messes. And God used every single one of them to change the world.

The common thread wasn't their ability—it was their availability. At some point, each of them said yes. Yes to the call. Yes to the risk. Yes to the unknown. They stopped waiting until they felt ready, and they started moving.

I love the old saying that God doesn't call the qualified—He qualifies the called. It captures something essential about how He works. You don't need to have all the answers before you take the next step. You don't need to feel confident. You don't need to understand how everything will work out.

You just need to say yes.

Maybe you've been waiting for a sign. Maybe you've been waiting for more clarity. Maybe you've been waiting until your circumstances are better, until you have more time, until you feel more spiritual. Maybe you've been waiting until the Jordan parts before you step in.

What if the sign you're waiting for is the invitation itself?

What if God has already spoken clearly enough, and now He's simply waiting for your response?

The invitation has been extended. Follow Me. Leave the nets. Take up your cross. Lose your life to find it. Love one another. Go and make disciples. Be salt and light.

What more clarity do you need?

A shepherd boy named David didn't wait until he was trained in combat before running toward Goliath. A teenage girl named Mary didn't wait until she understood reproductive biology before saying yes to an angel. Fishermen on a Galilean shore didn't wait until they'd completed a discipleship course before dropping their nets.

They just said yes. And God did the rest.

That same invitation is extended to you right now. Not to perfect performance, but to transforming relationship. Not to a life you've mastered, but to a journey you're beginning. Not to certainty, but to faith.

Will you say yes?

What's at Stake

Before you answer, I want you to understand what's at stake. Not to pressure you—but because your yes matters more than you might realize.

The world is watching.

I know that sounds dramatic, but it's true. People around you—in your neighborhood, at your workplace, in your extended family, scrolling past you on social media—are looking for evidence that God is real. They're looking for proof that life has meaning, that transformation is possible, that there's hope beyond the emptiness they feel.

They may not be sitting in church pews asking spiritual questions. But they're asking them in other ways. They're wondering why their success feels hollow. They're wondering why their relationships keep falling apart. They're wondering why they have everything the culture says they should want and still feel a gnawing sense that something essential is missing.

These people aren't going to read theological books or listen to apologetics podcasts. Most of them will never darken the door of a church on their own initiative.

But they're watching you.

They're watching how you handle stress. They're noticing whether your peace is real or just a performance. They're paying attention to how you treat the waitress, how you respond when things go wrong, how you talk about people who disagree with you. They're wondering whether your faith makes any actual difference.

Your bold yes could be the catalyst for someone else's salvation. Your surrendered life could be the model that shows them transformation is possible. Your courage to follow Jesus publicly could be the encouragement someone else needs to take their own first step.

When you live as a surrendered disciple—when your faith isn't just a Sunday activity but a Monday-through-Saturday reality—you become a signpost pointing to Jesus. You become evidence that He's real, that He's present, that He actually changes lives.

And here's the flip side: when we settle for cultural Christianity, we actually do harm. We become exhibit A for why faith doesn't matter. We confirm every suspicion skeptics have about religious hypocrisy. We make it easier for people to dismiss Jesus because the people who claim to follow Him don't seem any different from anyone else.

I don't say that to heap guilt on you. There is already enough guilt-tripping in the world. But I want you to understand that your choice matters. Your yes has implications beyond your own spiritual life. You are part of a chain that stretches back to those first disciples and forward to generations not yet born.

Someone said yes to the gospel so that you could hear it. Someone took a risk, shared their faith, lived out their convictions in front of you—and here you are. Now it's your turn. Future generations of your family, your community, your world are depending on disciples today who will stop dabbling and start following for real.

What's at stake? Everything. Your purpose. Your legacy. The people God has positioned you to reach. The story that will be told about your life when you're gone.

That's what's at stake.

The Promise: He Goes With You

Now I want you to hear something equally important: you don't do this alone.

The call to discipleship is a call to adventure, to risk, to stepping out of comfort zones. I've spent this whole book inviting you into something that will cost you. But I would be telling you only half the truth if I left you thinking you're on your own.

When God commissioned Joshua to lead the people into the Promised Land, He gave him a command and a promise. The command was clear: "Be strong and courageous. Do not be afraid; do not be discouraged." But the promise was even better: "For the Lord your God will be with you wherever you go."

Wherever you go. Not "in certain approved locations." Not "when things are going well." Not "as long as you don't mess up." Wherever you go.

Jesus made the same promise to His disciples at the end of Matthew's Gospel. After giving them the Great Commission—go and make disciples of all nations—He added words that must have taken their breath away: "And surely I am with you always, to the very end of the age."

Always. Not usually. Not most of the time. Always. To the very end of the age.

When God calls you forward, He doesn't send you by yourself. He doesn't point to the Jordan and say, "Good luck—hope it works out." He walks into the water with you. He goes ahead of you. He stands beside you. He has your back.

This is why Jesus sent the Holy Spirit. Before ascending to heaven, He told His disciples not to leave Jerusalem until they had received "the gift my Father promised." That gift was the Holy Spirit—the presence of God Himself dwelling inside His people.

The Spirit empowers what we could never do on our own. He guides us when we don't know the way. He comforts us when the journey gets hard. He convicts us when we drift off course. He equips us with exactly what we need for whatever God calls us to do.

You're not stepping into the water alone. You're stepping in with the Creator of the universe walking beside you. You're stepping in with two thousand years of saints cheering you on. You're stepping in with a promise that has never once failed.

Those priests at the Jordan—they didn't part the waters. They just got their feet wet. God did the parting. And God will do the parting in your life too. Your job is to step in. His job is everything else.

So, take courage. Not courage rooted in your own strength—that will fail you eventually. But courage rooted in His presence. He's already there. He's already working. He's already prepared the way.

You just need to step in.

A Prayer of Surrender

I want to offer you a prayer. It's not a magic formula. It's not a ritual that automatically changes everything the moment you say the words. But it's a way to put into language that your heart may be feeling—a way to make concrete the decision this book has been leading toward.

If you're ready—or even if you're just ready to be ready—I invite you to make these words your own. Pray them out loud if you can. There's something about speaking words that makes them feel more real, more committed, more like a covenant.

Lord Jesus,

I don't want to be a cultural Christian anymore. I don't want faith that's just a Sunday habit, a family tradition, a comfortable add-on to a life I'm running on my own terms. I want something more. I want something real. I believe that there is more.

I want to know You—not just know about You. I want to follow You—not just believe in You. I want my life to be defined by Your purposes, not my preferences.

So, I surrender. I surrender my plans—the ones I've made without asking You. I surrender my fears—the ones that have kept me playing it safe when You were calling me to risk. I surrender my comfort—the security I've built that has become more important to me than obedience. I surrender my future—whatever it holds, I want to hold it with open hands.

Make me into the disciple You created me to be. Use my life for Your glory. Take the ordinary pieces of who I am and weave them into Your extraordinary story.

Give me courage to say yes to whatever You call me to do. Give me faith to trust You when I can't see the path ahead. Give me endurance to keep following when the journey gets hard.

I'm stepping into the water. Meet me there. Part whatever needs to be parted. Provide whatever I lack. Be with me wherever You lead.

Not my will, but Yours be done.

Amen.

If you prayed that prayer and meant it—welcome to the adventure. Everything changes now. Not necessarily your circumstances, but your focus. Not necessarily your problems, but your perspective. You've stepped into the water. Now watch what God does.

And if you're not ready to pray it yet—that's okay. God is patient. He's not going anywhere. But don't let this book become just another good idea you read and forgot. Keep wrestling. Keep asking. Keep the door open.

He's still calling. The invitation still stands.

A Great Cloud of Witnesses

I want to close with a picture that has encouraged me more times than I can count.

In the eleventh chapter of Hebrews, the writer takes us on a tour of the faithful. He walks us through Israel's history, pointing out person after person who said yes to God against impossible odds. Abel. Enoch. Noah. Abraham. Sarah. Isaac. Jacob. Moses. Rahab. Gideon. Barak. Samson. David.

Some of these people conquered kingdoms and shut the mouths of lions. Others were tortured and refused to be released. Some escaped the edge of the sword. Others were put to death by the sword. Some received their dead raised back to life. Others were sawn in two.

The chapter doesn't sanitize their stories, or pretend faith leads to easy outcomes. It's honest about the cost. But it's also insistent about the value. These men and women were "commended for their faith," the writer tells us. They lived for something bigger than themselves. They trusted a promise they hadn't yet received.

Then comes chapter twelve, and the picture shifts. Having paraded these heroes before us, the writer issues a challenge:

"Therefore, since we are surrounded by such a great cloud of witnesses, let us throw off everything that hinders and the sin that so easily entangles. And let us run with perseverance the race marked out for us, fixing our eyes on Jesus, the pioneer and perfecter of faith."

Do you see what he's saying? We're not running alone. We're surrounded. The arena is packed with people who have run this race before us—and finished well. They're not spectators yelling from a safe distance. They're witnesses. They've been where we are. They know what it takes. And they're cheering us on.

Abraham is there, the man who left Ur with nothing but a promise. He's watching. Moses is there, the stutterer who faced down Pharaoh. He's watching. David is there, the shepherd boy who became a king. Ruth is there. Rahab is there. Mary and Peter and Paul are there.

And not just the biblical heroes. Every faithful follower who has run this race in the centuries since—they're part of the cloud too. The martyrs who died in Roman arenas rather than deny Christ. The missionaries who carried the gospel to the ends of the earth. The ordinary believers who lived extraordinary lives of faithfulness in quiet places no one remembers.

Your grandmother who prayed for you before you were born. The pastor who taught you about Jesus when you were a child. The friend who wouldn't give up on you when you had wandered far from faith.

They're all watching. They're all cheering. They're all saying, "You can do this. We did it—and you can too. The God who saw us through will see you through. Keep running. Don't give up. The finish line is worth it."

And at the center of it all, the One we're actually running toward: Jesus. The pioneer who blazed this trail before us. The perfecter who will complete the faith He started in us. We run toward Him. We run for Him. We run with our eyes fixed on Him.

You're not alone. You're not the first person to feel scared and inadequate and unsure if you have what it takes. Millions have felt exactly what you're feeling—and they stepped into the water anyway. They said yes. They ran the race. They finished well.

Now it's your turn.

The cloud is watching. The race is marked out. The pioneer has gone ahead.

Run.

The Life That Awaits

The life of a surrendered disciple is the most fulfilling life available to any human being.

It's not the easiest life. I won't lie to you about that. Following Jesus will cost you. The cross wasn't comfortable, and neither is carrying one daily.

But here's what I've discovered: easy and fulfilling are not the same thing. Some of the easiest seasons of my life have been the emptiest. And some of the hardest seasons have been the most meaningful.

There's a quality of life that comes from surrendered discipleship that nothing else produces. A sense of purpose that doesn't depend on circumstances. A peace that doesn't evaporate when problems arrive. A joy that persists even through pain. A confidence that you're part of something eternal, something that will matter long after you're gone.

I've watched people who have everything the world says you need—money, success, comfort, security—and they're miserable. And I've watched people who have almost nothing by worldly standards—but they have Jesus, and they're more alive than anyone I know.

The surrendered life is not the safe life. It's not the predictable life. But it's the life you were created for. And nothing else will satisfy.

Augustine understood this years ago when he wrote that our hearts are restless until they rest in God. That restlessness you may have felt as you've read this book—that holy discontent with a faith that doesn't transform, religion that doesn't satisfy, a Christianity that doesn't cost anything—that restlessness is a gift. It's God's way of saying there's more. So much more.

The more is available to you right now. Not someday. Not when you've got it figured out. Not when the circumstances are better. Now.

God is calling you to an adventure that will stretch you, challenge you, and remake you from the inside out. He's calling you to purpose that transcends your career, meaning that outlasts your circumstances, and joy that sustains you through suffering.

He's calling you to follow Him.

The question before you is simple: Will you say yes?

A Final Word

A missionary from another era once wrote something that has stayed with me for years. He observed that we have only one life, and it will soon be past—and when it's over, only what's done for Christ will last.

It's a sobering thought, isn't it? One life. That's all we get. Every day that passes is one less day we have to make a difference, to love people well, to invest in eternity, to answer the call.

What are you doing with your one life?

I don't know what your Jordan River looks like. I don't know what step of faith God is asking you to take. Maybe it's a conversation you've been avoiding. Maybe it's a surrender you've been postponing. Maybe it's a dream you've been too scared to pursue. Maybe it's a call you've been pretending not to hear.

Whatever it is—the water is right in front of you.

The Jordan didn't part until the priests stepped in. The miracle followed the faith. The provision came after the obedience.

That's how God works. And He's waiting for you to step in.

The Great Commission is still great. The invitation is still open. The cloud of witnesses is still cheering. Jesus is still saying what He said two thousand years ago on the shores of Galilee:

Follow Me.

Will you?

———————————

"Now then, you and all these people, get ready to cross the Jordan River into the land I am about to give to them...

Be strong and courageous. Do not be afraid; do not be discouraged, for the Lord your God will be with you

wherever you go."

—*Joshua 1:2, 9 (NIV)*

20

Study Guide: Chapter Six

Personal Reflection Questions

Take time alone with these questions. Be honest. This is between you and God.

As you look back over this entire book, what has impacted you most? What truths, stories, or challenges have stayed with you? What has God been saying to you through these pages?

The priests had to step into the Jordan before the waters parted. What step of faith is God asking you to take right now—before you can see the way clear? Be specific.

Write down your "bold yes" to God. What specific commitment are you making as a result of reading this book? Don't write something vague like "I'll try harder." Write something concrete and measurable.

What fears or obstacles still stand between you and full surrender? Name them honestly. Then bring them to God in prayer—not asking Him to remove them necessarily, but asking for courage to move forward despite them.

Hebrews 11-12 speaks of a "great cloud of witnesses." Who in your life has modeled surrendered discipleship for you? What did you learn from watching them? How will you pass that legacy on to others?

Group Discussion Questions

For small groups, Sunday school classes, or discussion with a trusted friend.

Share with the group: What is your key takeaway from this book? How has your understanding of discipleship changed since you started reading? What do you see differently now?

Read Joshua 3:7-17 together. What principles can we draw from this story about stepping out in faith? Why do you think God designed it so the water didn't part until the priests stepped in? What does that teach us about how faith works?

Discuss the statement: "God doesn't call the qualified—He qualifies the called." How have you seen this play out in your own life or the lives of others? How does this truth affect your willingness to say yes to God?

What does "the bold yes" look like practically for your group? Is there something God might be calling you to do together as a result of this study? A ministry initiative? A community impact? A shared commitment?

How will you hold each other accountable to the commitments made through this study? What structures, rhythms, or practices will help you stay on track? Who will check in with whom, and how often?

Action Step

This week, make your commitment concrete. Take three specific actions:

First, write a letter to yourself describing the surrendered disciple you want to become and the specific steps you're committing to take. Be honest about where you are now, clear about where you want to be, and specific about how you'll get there. Seal the letter and then return to it in six months.

Second, identify your accountability—the person or group who will walk with you as you pursue surrendered discipleship. Contact them this week. Tell them what you've committed to. Give them permission to ask hard questions. If you haven't formed a Discipleship Band – now is a great time.

Third, take one immediate step toward your bold yes—something you can do today, not someday. Have the conversation. Make the call. Start the practice. Give the gift. Say the words. Don't let this book become another good intention you never acted on. The Jordan is in front of you. Step in.

In six months, when you revisit your letter, evaluate honestly: Am I living as a surrendered disciple, or have I slipped back into cultural Christianity? Use it as a checkpoint to recalibrate and recommit.

Remember: this isn't the end of the journey—it's just the beginning. The life of a surrendered disciple is lived one day at a time, one decision at a time, one yes at a time. You don't have to be perfect. You just have to keep following.

The cloud of witnesses is watching. The Spirit is empowering. Jesus is leading.

Go.

The journey continues...

"Follow Me."

—*Jesus Christ*

EPILOGUE

A Word Before You Go

Before you close this book and step back into your life, I want to share one more thing with you.

Over the years, I've learned that the moment after a decision is often more important than the decision itself. It's easy to feel inspired while you're reading. It's easy to pray a prayer of surrender in a quiet moment. The real test comes tomorrow morning when the alarm goes off, the inbox fills up, the kids need breakfast, and the demands of ordinary life crowd back in.

That's when cultural Christianity whispers its familiar invitation: "You can get serious about this later. Right now, just get through the day."

Don't listen.

The surrendered life isn't built in dramatic moments—it's built in ordinary ones. It's built in the first decision you make when your feet hit the floor. It's built in how you treat your spouse before you've had your coffee. It's built in the attitude you carry into work, the patience you show in traffic, the way you respond when someone lets you down.

Discipleship is daily. That's what makes it hard. But that's also what makes it real.

So, here's what I want you to know as you go:

You will stumble. I can promise you that. You'll have days when you forget everything you've read in these pages. You'll fall back into old patterns. You'll catch yourself checking boxes instead of pursuing Jesus. You'll wonder if you're really cut out for this surrendered disciple thing.

When that happens—and it will—don't quit. Don't assume your failure disqualifies you. Don't let the enemy convince you that because you stumbled, you might as well stop running.

Get up. Dust off. Start again.

Peter denied Jesus three times, and Jesus restored him three times. David's sins were spectacular failures, yet God called him a man after His own heart. The same grace that saved you is the grace that sustains you. It's new every morning.

You are not alone. Find your people. Lock arms with a few fellow travelers who will walk this road with you—who will encourage you when you're weary, challenge you when you're drifting, and celebrate with you when you see God move. The Christian life was never meant to be lived in isolation. You need the body, and the body needs you. Go to worship on Sundays. (I know it's easier to watch while wearing your pajamas and drinking coffee in bed – but get up, get ready, and go.) Join a Sunday school class and/or a small group – get to know people at a different level. Form a Discipleship Band – a group of 3-5 men or women who meet regularly to support each other in pursuing the "more" that Christ has to offer. Find a way to serve – be the hands and feet of Christ to someone else – join in His mission in our world.

Small steps matter. You don't have to transform your entire life by next Tuesday. You just need to take the next faithful step. Have the conversation you've been avoiding. Open your Bible before you open your phone. Serve someone who can't repay you. Speak an encouraging word. Give when it stretches you. One step leads to another, and before you know it, you're on a journey you never imagined.

God is for you. Not against you. Not disappointed in you. Not waiting for you to earn His approval. He delights in you. He's cheering you on. He's working in ways you can't see to shape you into the person He created you to be. Trust His heart, even when you can't trace His hand.

I've had the privilege of watching so many people make the journey from cultural Christian to surrendered disciple. Some of them had dramatic conversion stories; most didn't. Some of them went on to do things the world would call remarkable; most served faithfully in ways that will never make headlines. But every single one of them would tell you the same thing: it was worth it. Every cost, every sacrifice, every uncomfortable step of obedience—worth it.

The abundant life Jesus promised isn't found in having more. It's found in surrendering more. And the deeper you go with Him, the more you realize that what you thought you were giving up was never really yours to begin with.

So, go. Step into the water. Say yes to whatever God puts in front of you today. Be salt and light wherever you find yourself. Make your world better and brighter. Love the people He's placed in your path. Live like you actually believe what you say you believe.

The world doesn't need more cultural Christians. It has plenty of those.

The world needs surrendered disciples who will follow Jesus into the mess, carry hope into the darkness, and demonstrate by their lives that God is real and His kingdom is coming.

The world needs you.

May the God who called you also equip you.

May the Christ who saved you also send you.

May the Spirit who dwells in you also empower you.

And may you discover, in the beautiful adventure of following Jesus, that you were made for so much more than Sunday.

With you on the journey,

Bill

"Now to him who is able to do immeasurably more
than all we ask or imagine,
according to his power that is at work within us,
to him be glory in the church and in Christ Jesus
throughout all generations, for ever and ever!
Amen."
— *Ephesians 3:20-21 (NIV)*

DISCIPLESHIP BANDS

Time + Trust = Transformation

A Discipleship Band is a group of three to five men or women who meet weekly or bi-weekly to engage in transformational questions and to pray for one another. These groups can be in person or virtual.

When your Discipleship Band meets, you follow this format:
Opening

Prayer: Our Father, thank you for this time set aside to reflect on your goodness and faithfulness. Thank you for giving us each other to share our lives with, that we might better understand how your Spirit is moving and working in your disciples gathered here. Holy Spirit, abide with us and speak through us, so that in all things you may be glorified. In Jesus name we pray, Amen.

Questions:

Each person takes time to share around the questions below:
How have you seen and experienced God in your life this week?
What have been your struggles and/or successes?
How can we help you, encourage you, and pray for you?
When you are ready to go deeper:
How is God's Word and the Holy Spirit speaking in your life?

What do you feel God is calling you to do?

When each person has finished sharing, allow time for prayer.

Closing

Prayer: Our Lord, You are faithful in all things, and we pray this Scripture as a reminder of the unconditional love found in relationship with you. Equip us to speak boldly of your promises and walk humbly in your presence. "Now to Him who is able to do immeasurably more than all we ask or imagine, according to His power that is at work within us, to Him be glory in the church and in Christ Jesus throughout all generations, for ever and ever! Amen." (Ephesians 3:20-21)

21

ABOUT THE AUTHOR

Dr. Bill Brunson is the Senior Pastor of Vestavia Hills Methodist Church in Birmingham, Alabama, where he leads a thriving congregation of over 3,400 members. With more than thirty-five years of ministry experience, Bill has dedicated his life to helping people move from simply believing in Jesus to actually following Him.

Known for his engaging storytelling, practical wisdom, and contagious passion for transformation, Bill brings a unique blend of biblical depth and real-world application to everything he teaches.

Bill is also a John Maxwell Certified Coach and DISC Consultant and a Jon Gordon Certified Positive Leader.

For information on coaching, DISC Consultation, or speaking for groups and events – Bill can be reached through DeeperPurposeCoaching.com and bill@deeperpurposecoaching.com

Bill lives in Hoover, Alabama, with his wife Michelle.

ALSO BY DR. BILL BRUNSON

Faith, Leadership, and Walt:
Leading with Purpose, Passion, and the Power of Possibility
Help and Hope:
A Devotional by a Caregiver for Caregivers